THE
COUNTRY
MOTHERS

*A Celebration of Motherhood
and Old-fashioned Cooking*

COOKBOOK

For Cathy—

Jane Watson Hopping

Enjoy these old-time memories!

THE
COUNTRY
MOTHERS

*A Celebration of Motherhood
and Old-fashioned Cooking*

COOKBOOK

JANE WATSON HOPPING

VILLARD BOOKS · NEW YORK · 1991

Grateful acknowledgment is made to the following for permission to reprint previously published material:
Contemporary Books, Inc.: Fourteen poems from *Collected Verse of Edgar A. Guest*. Copyright 1934. Reprinted by arrangement with Contemporary Books, Inc., Chicago.
The Kansas City Star Co.: "A Woman's Prayer." Reprinted by permission.
Music Sales Corporation: "Billy Boy" and "Cradle Song" from *Everybody's Favorite Community Songs*. Used by permission of Music Sales Corp. International Copyright Secured. All Rights Reserved.

Library of Congress Cataloging-in-Publication Data

Hopping, Jane Watson.
   The country mother's cookbook: a celebration of motherhood and old-fashioned cooking/by Jane Watson Hopping.
      p.   cm.
   Includes index.
   ISBN 0-394-58874-6
   1. Cookery, American.   I. Title.
TX715.H7866 1991
641.5973—dc20   90-44723

DESIGNED BY BARBARA MARKS

Manufactured in the United States of America

9   8   7   6   5   4   3   2

First edition

For devoted mothers everywhere,
especially my own

Acknowledgments

THIS COOKBOOK IS A tribute to all those whose hands have rocked the cradle, and to the children whose lives the *motherly touch* has enriched. It has been for me a journey of the heart, a close and sharing time with my mother, who dipped deep into her childhood memories for recollections, anecdotes, bits of gentle wisdom. Out of her past vividly came the *Spring Thaw: A Tale About Foxes* and *An Old-Time Mother's Day Picnic.*

Others, to whom I would like to express gratitude, are those who have shared their thoughts and recollections, lending warmth to the book: Herman and Vera Kamping, Meg Ruley, Aunt Mabel Porter, Grandma Hopping, and Grandma White.

As always, I would like to thank Sheila, my sister, for the decorative art, particularly the flowers, which bring a lovely continuity to the whole. And Raymond, my husband, who supports my efforts, constantly and in many ways. I must mention here, my great-grandnephew, Cris, and dear friends Rachel, Naomi, and baby Hannah, who often have sent my mothering juices to flowing so abundantly that they have yielded up more than one story or anecdote for the cookbook.

Here a word of gratitude to all of the poets whose beautiful songs have graced the pages of the book.

Many thanks to Alison Acker and Emily Bestler, supportive editors to whom I owe much, Nancy Inglis, copy editor, Thomas G. Fiffer, Arne Rickert and Corinne Lewkowicz for skills they have brought to the work, and all of the talented folk at Villard Books who gave their best to it.

Many blessings to Meg Ruley, and thanks to everyone at The Jane Rotrosen Agency.

And a sincere thank you to readers for the warm letters, kind words, and encouragement you have showered on me.

From THE RAGGEDY MAN ON CHILDREN

CHILDREN—take 'em as they run—
  You kin *bet* on ev'ry one!—
Treat 'em right and reco'nize
Human souls is all one size.

Jevver think?—the world's best men
Wears the same souls they had when
They run barefoot—'way back where
All these little children air.

—James Whitcomb Riley

Contents

The Old House by the Side of the Road
98

SIMPLE THINGS AND COMMON FOLKS
100

Aunt Mabel's Brown Stew

Old-fashioned Collops

Auntie's Squabs with Green Peas

MA LOVES ME WHEN I'M GOOD OR BAD
91

Ma's Layered Meat Loaf

Baked Potatoes with Dill Butter

Fancy Buttered Carrots

LONG AGO
95

Soft Molasses Hermits

An Old-Time Mother's Day Picnic
105

AN EMBARRASSMENT OF CARP
112

Creamed Carp and Carp à la Chambord

Deviled Salmon with Medium White Sauce and Mashed-Potato Meringue

Effie's Broiled Fish with Parsley and Lemon Butter

Old-fashioned Soused Fish

Mother's Day
119

LITTLE GIRL, O SO SWEET
121

Ann's Easy-to-Make Star Cookies

Young Elizabeth's Fruit and Nut Chocolate Icebox Cookies

Nelly's First Cupcakes

Knee-deep in June
125

HER SMILE OF CHEER AND VOICE OF LOVE
127

Little Darlin' Cookies

STRAWBERRIES, SOFT CHEEKS TURNED TO THE SUN
130

Ada's Old-Time Strawberry Shortcake

Effie's Easy-to-Make Strawberry-Preserve Roll

Aunt Irene's Fresh Strawberry Sherbet with Almond Cluster Cookies

Month of Roses, Month of Bees, and Month of Brides
139

NOW THE SUN IS SHINING, AND THERE ARE ROSES EVERYWHERE
140

Rose-Blossom Tea

Dried Rosebuds

Rose-Petal Vinegar

OLD JOHN
208

Grandma Hoskin's Red-Rose Honey

Old-fashioned Coffee Cakes

*Mrs. Hovin's White Cake with
Seven-Minute Frosting*

There's Somethin' About October
214

A-LIVIN' ALL ALONE THERE IN THAT LONESOME SORT O' WAY
215

Venison Pot Roast with Vegetables

*Baked Acorn Squash Topped with
Toasted Peanuts*

Mock Oysters

Gentle Memories of Home
220

THE FARM SECURITY LOAN
222

Vera's Apple Dumplings

THE GOBBLE-UNS'LL GIT YOU EF YOU DON'T WATCH OUT!
226

Ada's Toasted English Walnuts

*Delicious Glazed Ham Balls
in a Nooodle Ring*

Crunchy D'Anjou Pear Salad

Effie's Coconut-Custard Pie

NUTS, SQUIRRELS, AND PECAN PIES
232

*Slivered Almonds and Dried Apricot
Nut Bread*

*Mother's Baked Apple Pudding with
Toasted English Walnuts and Brandy
Sauce*

Easy-to-Make Pecan Pie

THE HOME AT PEACE

HERE is a little world where children play
   And just a few red roses greet July;
   Above it smiles God's stretch of summer sky;
Here laughter rings to mark the close of day;
There is no greater splendor far away.
   Here slumber comes with all her dream
      supply,
   And friendship visits as the days go by;
Here love and faith keep bitterness at bay.
Should up this walk come wealth or smiling fame,
   Some little treasures might be added here,
But life itself would still remain the same:
   Love is no sweeter in a larger sphere.
This little world of ours wherein we live
Holds now the richest joys which life can give.

               —Edgar A. Guest

Introduction:
Drifting on the River of Time

DURING THE THIRTIES, EXCEPT for the seasons our family spent farming on the old Hubbard place, we lived in a small cabin deep in the American River canyon on Sugar Rock Quarry property in northern California. For me, there will always be something magical about those years. Perhaps it's because we were in gold country near Coloma and the relics of those times were richly about us. Or perhaps it was only a child's love for the tiny cabin with wild flowers and wild game that came right up to the back door.

It was a quiet place, the air cool and fresh. Around us the tree-studded mountains rose up to shut out the rest of the world. In summer Mother's petunias, cosmos, and phlox bloomed in profusion in the yard and soft breezes wafted down the canyon. In winter the mountains protected us from wind and weather. And in part they sheltered us from the raging economic storms that swept the country and laid waste to so many lives.

All through those early years, during my childhood and my sister's, our mother was there, moving back and forth, scrubbing floors and counters, putting flowers on the table, teasing us and letting us spoon bits of good things out of the bowls from which she was cooking. We were warm, dry and well fed. In time, Grandpa, our mother's father, who lived with us, would come in from chopping wood and settle down in an oak and leather chair he had made for himself from the rumble seat of an old car to smoke his pungent pipe and talk a bit with Mother about work that needed to be done, fishing, or gardening.

While they visited in the comfortable way that people do who have shared much and many years together, Mother finished up supper. Eventually our father would come back from a summer day's work or from walking his trap lines in winter. Always, Mother went to the door to greet him, pulling him into the shelter of home and family. She taught us all to respect him. He was a loyal husband and loving father. All their married life, Mother laid aside the best slices of meat from the middle of the roast for him, put the first freshly made doughnuts on his plate, and sewed shirts for him that brought out the blue of his eyes, fitting the sleeves to his arms alone. When asked about such things, her only explanation was that he deserved it.

Today, looking at photographs of those years—the late twenties through the late thirties—one might think we were poor. It would be hard to guess that the folks in cotton dresses and stretched-out sweaters, heavy boots and rough

coats were not in desperate straits, for a faded photograph could hardly tell of the wealth of family, of loving aunts and uncles, of sharing and security. Nor could it show the inner strength of such people; their stiff backs, the defiant spirits that laughed, made music, went square dancing, recited poetry, played cards and baseball right in the face of adversity. And it could not speak of the pride they took in their self-sufficiency, or of the skills with which they took care of their own.

From treasured memories drawn out of those times, and from family stories that reach even further into the past, have come this book, *The Country Mothers Cookbook*. While it is about old-time folks of every persuasion, it is primarily about down-home cooking and old-fashioned mothering, about aunts and well-loved old women with names like Aunt Fanny and Ol' Missus Upjohn, the widow Boyle, and Mama Lowery.

There are a few sad songs in this book—because life consists of joyful times and hard ones—and many stories of old-time people and their acts of love and courage. It is very definitely about motherhood and the special bond between mother and child. It's about the reassuring touch of a mother's hands, the warmth of her body, and the beat of her heart, the outpouring of wonder and love that binds each new infant to this world, nurturing the spirit as surely as breast milk strengthens the body. It's about growing up in the country in a different time. About growing old and seeing your babies become men and women of worth. And it is about marriages that last for fifty years.

For the most part, though, it is about good wholesome country food that is easy to prepare and for which ingredients are not costly. Some recipes are a little spoofy, such as Creamed Carp, and some are fantastic, such as Old-Fashioned Daffodil Tarts with Cookie Crust and Cloud Light Gelatin Pudding.

Included are a few family-size recipes, such as Colleen's Favorite Sugar Cookies, Grandma King's Patty-Pan Bread and A Crowd-Pleasing Apple Dessert. To impress the menfolk, there are recipes like Amethyst Raspberry Tarts with Cookie Crust, An Old-Fashioned One-Two-Three-Four Cake with Lemon Filling and Whipped Snow Frosting.

When I bake one of the well-loved cakes or make any of the other dishes that appeared regularly on our family tables, memories flood over me. Some of the handed-down recipes are generations old. Others are those I developed to please my own family. And still others, those I consider a part of our national culinary tradition, are tucked away in the book because women of the past swore by them and won prizes at country fairs with them.

The chapters begin deep in January during the lingering days of winter and end with the coming of the new year, celebrating not only the seasonal flow of the countryside, but, because country people live so close to the earth, the surging flow of human existence as well. Through art, poetry, stories, and oral histories, the daily lives of simple rural folk are revealed: the hard-won success of men and women who struggle against odds to provide for their families, the tender watchfulness over the aging, and the joy-filled renewal of birth.

As I wrote this book, I hoped that the warmth of it might evoke visions of strong, old-fashioned families, might set each of us to reminiscing about a well-remembered kitchen filled with the aroma of home-cooked food, that we might fondly recall our own mother's gentle words of wisdom and count again all of the golden threads that she wove into the fabric of our lives.

From MOTHER

WORDS cannot tell what this old heart would say of her,
Mother—the sweetest and fairest of all.

—Edgar A. Guest

From MARJORIE'S ALMANAC

APPLES in the orchard
   Mellowing one by one;
Strawberries upturning
   Soft cheeks to the sun;
Roses faint with sweetness,
   Lilies fair of face,
Drowsy scents and murmurs
   Haunting every place;
Lengths of golden sunshine,
   Moonlight bright as day—
Don't you think that summer's
   Pleasanter than May?

—Thomas Bailey Aldrich

From THE ALL-GOLDEN

I catch my breath as children do
In woodland swings when life is new
And all the blood is warm as wine
And tingles with a tang divine.

My soul soars up the atmosphere
And sings aloud where God can hear,
And all my being leans intent
To mark His smiling wonderment.
O gracious dream, and gracious time,

And gracious theme, and gracious rhyme—
When buds of Spring begin to blow
In blossoms that we used to know
And lure us back along the ways
Of time's all-golden yesterdays!

—James Whitcomb Riley

THE
COUNTRY
MOTHERS

A Celebration of Motherhood
and Old-fashioned Cooking

COOKBOOK

The Low, Mysterious Laughter of the Rain

THE LAUGHTER OF THE RAIN

The rain sounds like a laugh to me—
A low laugh poured out limpidly.

My very soul smiles as I listen to
   The low, mysterious laughter of the rain,
   Poured musically over heart and brain
Till sodden care, soaked with it through and through,
Sinks; and, with wings wet with it as with dew,
   My spirit flutters up, with every stain
   Rinsed from its plumage, and as white again
As when the old laugh of the rain was new.
   Then laugh on, happy Rain! laugh louder yet!—
Laugh out in torrent-bursts of watery mirth;
   Unlock thy lips of purple cloud, and let
Thy liquid merriment baptize the earth,
   And wash the sad face of the world, and set
   The universe to music dripping-wet!

—James Whitcomb Riley

In January, on late winter days when clouds were heavy and dark, when rain poured down over hillsides, eroding gullies that exposed the earth, country people eventually got cabin fever from being cooped up inside. Children got fussy and restless, men got tired of fixing and mending, and women spent much time trying to entertain and ease the boredom by making cookies with the children.

In time a nearby relative or neighbor would hitch up the team, pile his well-bundled family in the wagon, and brave the rut-deep muddy roads to go visitin'. Despite the heavy wraps and blankets they would arrive soaked but happy, coming in out of the storm with smiling faces and boisterous greetings. Some came with a banjo, guitar, mandolin, or fiddle wrapped in an oilskin and a blanket, ready to stay a while and play a few tunes. At their mother's instruction, young girls would run down to the cellar or out to the apple house and bring back a huge bread-bowl filled with winter-stored apples—Winesaps, Arkansas Blacks, Northern Spy, and others—and enough popcorn to pop a large clean dishpan full.

Soon the party was in full swing. The women visited, heads close together, while the menfolk tapped out a rhythm to the lively music—"Froggy Went a Courtin'," "Sourwood Mountain," "El-a-noy" (a song of the pioneers). They also played "Red River Valley," a lovely song adapted long ago by Western folk from the original version called "In the Bright Mohawk Valley," whose authors loved the Mohawk Valley hills of New York State. Musically inclined little ones pranced about, beating in time to the music on a tin pan with a stick of kindling, and when there was a pause in the music, men—uncles or fond friends—would tell the little ones, "You're doing fine. You play pretty good."

Then as the afternoon waned, the children were wrapped in blankets which had dried by the fire, and a lingering good-bye was taken by all, with promises of another visit soon.

THE COUNTRY MOTHERS COOKBOOK

Violets, Violets Everywhere

IN FEBRUARY AND EARLY March, the earth awakens from a deep winter slumber, violets unfurl again their sweet-scented magic, spreading their flowery blankets over the lush new grass in the yard, out under trees not yet budded out and in the pasture behind the barn.

SUN AND RAIN

ALL day the sun and rain have been as friends,
    Each vying with the other which shall be
    Most generous in dowering earth and sea
With their glad wealth, till each, as it descends,
Is mingled with the other, where it blends
    In one warm, glimmering mist that falls on me
    As once God's smile fell over Galilee.
The lily-cup, filled with it, droops and bends
    Like some white saint beside a sylvan shrine
In silent prayer; the roses at my feet,
    Baptized with it as with a crimson wine,
Gleam radiant in grasses grown so sweet,
    The blossoms lift, with tenderness divine,
    Their wet eyes heavenward with these of mine.

—James Whitcomb Riley

JANE WATSON HOPPING

Out Under the Maple Tree

GRANDPARENTS PLAY SUCH AN important role in a child's life. They bring to it continuity with the past, closeness, emotional comfort, and enrichment. They generously give insight into life and teach rules for successful living. It's as though the old and young, living as they do in the spring and winter of life, have much more in common than those who are struggling through the heavy tasks of summer and the fall harvest:

THE COUNTRY MOTHERS COOKBOOK

ONE, TWO, THREE

IT was an old, old, old, old lady,
   And a boy that was half-past three;
And the way that they played together
   Was beautiful to see.

She couldn't go running and jumping,
   And the boy, no more could he,
For he was a thin little fellow,
   With a thin little twisted knee.

They sat in the yellow sunlight
   Out under the maple tree;
And the game that they played I'll tell you
   Just as it was told to me.

It was Hide-and-go-seek they were playing,
   Though you'd never have known it to be—
With an old, old, old, old lady,
   And a boy with a twisted knee.

The boy would bend his face down
   On his one little sound right knee,
And he'd guess where she was hiding,
   In guesses One, Two, Three.

"You are in the china closet,"
   He would cry, and laugh with glee—
It wasn't the china closet;
   But he still had Two and Three.

"You are up in papa's big bedroom,
   In the chest with the queer old key."
And she said: "You are warm and warmer;
   But you're not quite right," said she.

"It can't be the little cupboard
   Where mamma's things used to be;
So it must be the clothes-press, grandma."
   And he found her with his Three.

Then she covered her face with her fingers,
   That were wrinkled and white and wee,
And she guessed where the boy was hiding,
   With a One and a Two and a Three.

And they never had stirred from their place
   Out under the maple tree—
This old, old, old, old lady
   And the boy with the lame little knee—
This dear, dear, dear old lady,
   And the boy who was half-past three.

          —H. C. Bunner

OLD-FAVORITE ICEBOX COOKIES

makes about 8 dozen cookies

THESE COOKIES BARELY KEEP, especially if there are several men and a gaggling of children about the place. They can, when necessary, be stored in a gallon glass jar which has a tight lid and be put on a top shelf.

2 cups sifted all-purpose flour
1½ teaspoons baking powder
½ teaspoon salt
½ cup butter or margarine,
   softened at room temperature

1 cup sugar
1 egg
1 cup shredded coconut
1 tablespoon milk
1 teaspoon vanilla extract

Into a medium bowl, sift flour with baking powder and salt. In a large bowl, cream butter with sugar until light. Then, add egg, coconut, milk, and vanilla, and beat well. Add flour *1 cup* at a time, mixing well after each addition.

Divide dough into two portions and roll each into a log 1½ inches in diameter. Roll each in waxed paper and refrigerate overnight, or until firm enough to slice.

Before baking, allow about 15 minutes to preheat oven to 425°F. Set out an ungreased baking sheet. Then, as oven heats, remove dough from refrigerator and lay logs on a lightly floured surface. Cut into ⅛-inch slices (¼-inch slices, if you prefer). Arrange unbaked cookies on baking sheet.

Bake until lightly browned, about 5 minutes (watch baking time carefully). When done, remove from oven and immediately lift with a spatula and put on brown paper to cool. Bake one batch after another until dough is used up.

Let Loose the Sails of Love

From AN OLD SWEETHEART OF MINE

WHEN I should be her lover forever and a day,
And she my faithful sweetheart till the golden hair was gray;
And we should be so happy that when either's lips were dumb
They would not smile in Heaven till the other's kiss had come.

—James Whitcomb Riley

SOMETIMES I THINK THAT Uncle Bud, a man with little formal schooling yet wise in the ways of living, understood better than most men the hearts of women. In a natural unspoiled way, he sensed their need to be noticed and appreciated. He kidded them gently, complimenting with just a few laughing words honestly meant, and women in turn liked and trusted him.

In the spring he would pick dainty wild flowers out of his fields or along the roadway and bring them home in a bearlike grip to Aunt Sue. When they got older, he would kiss her and call her Rosebud and tell her that the gray in her hair was the color of polished silver. On their fiftieth wedding anniversary, completely gray at nearly seventy, he gently picked her up, not even mussing up her new ivory lace dress, and carried her over the threshold of their home, just as he had done on their wedding day when she was still a slip of a girl.

JANE WATSON HOPPING

$\mathcal{L}$OVE KNOTS

makes 3 dozen love knots

AUNTIE LEARNED TO MAKE these little treats in the late twenties or early thirties. Uncle Bud thought there was "nothin' to beat 'em," so through the years Auntie has tied many love knots.

1 cup butter or margarine
2½ cups sifted cake flour
6 eggs, beaten to a froth
¼ cup heavy cream

1 teaspoon vanilla extract
1 cup sugar
½ teaspoon salt
Almond Icing (recipe follows)

In a large bowl, with a pastry blender, cut butter into flour. In a medium bowl, combine beaten eggs with cream, vanilla, sugar, and salt. Make a well in the butter-flour mixture, and stir egg mixture into the dry ingredients to form a ball of dough. Refrigerate to chill dough for about 20 minutes.

As dough chills, preheat oven to 350°F. Set out a baking sheet 15½ × 10½ × 1 inch (smaller baking sheets will do if you don't have a large one). Then on a lightly floured smooth surface, roll chilled dough into rolls about 6 inches long and as thick as a lead pencil. Shape into love knots; brush with Almond Icing and bake until golden around edges (nuts will be lightly toasted), about 12 to 15 minutes. Store in an airtight tin.

$\mathcal{A}$LMOND ICING

makes enough for 3 dozen love knots

1 egg white
1 tablespoon milk

3 tablespoons sugar
½ cup finely chopped almonds

Beat egg white slightly; add milk and sugar. Brush Love Knots with icing and sprinkle with almond bits.

$\mathcal{W}$EDDING-RING COOKIES

makes about 5 dozen cookies

AUNTIE LOVED THESE OLD-FASHIONED cookies and made them each year for Valentine's Day. Uncle Bud named them and ate them by the handfuls.

2¾ cups sifted all-purpose flour plus about ⅔ cup more for rolling out cookies
1 teaspoon salt
½ teaspoon soda
½ cup butter or margarine, softened at room temperature

1 cup dairy sour cream
1½ cups firmly packed light brown sugar
2 eggs, beaten to a froth
1 teaspoon vanilla extract
½ cup milk, slightly more if needed
Maple Butter Glaze (recipe follows)

Preheat oven to 350°F. Thoroughly grease a large baking sheet and set aside until needed.

Into a medium bowl, sift flour with salt and soda. Set aside. In a large bowl, cream butter, sour cream, and sugar together until light. Combine beaten eggs and vanilla and gradually add to butter mixture, stirring until well blended. Then alternately add milk and reserved flour mixture, stirring well after each addition. If the dough is soft, chill for 30 minutes before rolling.

Turn the dough onto a lightly floured surface and roll out to a thickness of ¼ to ½ inch. Cut into circles with a medium doughnut cutter and place 1 inch apart on prepared baking sheet.

Bake until light brown, about 7 to 10 minutes. Immediately remove from pan with a spatula and cool on a wire rack or on brown paper—an opened grocery bag will do nicely. While still slightly warm, glaze with Maple Butter Glaze.

MAPLE BUTTER GLAZE

makes about 1 cup

⅓ cup butter
2 cups powdered sugar

1½ teaspoons maple flavoring
2 to 4 tablespoons hot water

Melt butter in a saucepan. Blend in sugar and maple flavoring. Stir in water, 1 tablespoon at a time, until glaze is of a spreadable consistency.

TENDER KISSES

makes about 1 dozen generous size kisses

UNCLE BUD LOVED THESE airy, sweet kisses and Auntie made them for him in the spring when eggs were plentiful. And she teased him about them: he could eat these in a wink, barely leaving enough for the rest of the family.

6 egg whites
Pinch of salt

½ teaspoon cream of tartar
1½ cups sugar

Preheat oven to 250°F. Using a metal whisk, beat egg whites in a medium-size bowl until soft peaks form; add salt and cream of tartar. Gradually add sugar, beating constantly until stiff, moist peaks form. Cut a piece of heavy brown wrapping paper and place it on a cookie sheet. Using a large spoon, mound the egg-white mixture on the paper; take care to make the mounds of equal size. Bake for 1 hour, then turn off oven, leaving the kisses in the oven until they are cool.

Like a Rosebud Peeking at Me

IN OLD-FASHIONED FAMILIES LIKE ours, children were (and are) loved and held dear. For who could resist the laughter and playful ways of boys and girls, their invigorating companionship, and who in farm country could deny the strength brought to the family by their helping hands? Our great-grandmother had thirteen children, the first being born in Black Lick, Ohio, on the edge of the frontier, the last, my grandfather, born in Missouri in 1875. It is said in the family that she thought each child was the sweetest yet, and that those children who were still at home agreed with her and would gather around eagerly to join in, sharing love for the newest baby.

Some years ago when I found this lovely prayer, I thought of Great-Grandma and her many travails, and about her love for each of her children. And while I know these thoughts are not hers alone, I would like to share them here with you.

Baby Carolyn

JANE WATSON HOPPING

12

A WOMAN'S PRAYER
(For the Child to Come)

God, I am going down to find a little soul, a thing that shall be mine as no other thing in the world has been mine.

Keep me for my child's life. Bring me through my hour strong and well for the sake of my baby.

Prepare me for real motherhood. Preserve my mind from doubts, and worries, and all fearsome misgivings, that I may not stain my thoughts with cowardice, for my child's sake.

Drive all angers and impurities, all low and unworthy feelings from me, that the little mind that is forming may become a brave, clean wrestler in this world of dangers.

And, God, when the child lies in my arms, and draws his life from me, and when his eyes look up to mine, to learn what this new world is like, I pledge Thee the child shall find reverence in me, and no fear; truth and no shame; love strong as life and death, and no hates nor petulancies.

God, make my baby love me. I ask no endowments for excellencies for my child, but only that the place of motherhood, once given me, may never be taken from me. As long as the soul lives that I shall bring forth, let there be in it one secret shrine that shall always be mother's.

Give the child a right, clean mind, and a warm, free soul.

And I promise Thee that I shall study the child, and seek to find what gifts and graces Thou has implanted, and to develop them. I shall respect the child's personality.

I am but Thy little one, O Father. I fold my hands and put them between Thy hands, and say, "Give me a normal baby, and make me a normal mother."

Amen.

—Anonymous

THE WIDOW BOYLE'S SUNSHINE CAKE WITH A SIMPLE OLD-FASHIONED LEMON SAUCE

makes one 9-inch tube cake

THE WIDOW, AS EVERYONE called her, lived in a small cabin up in the hills of southwestern Missouri along the flow of Wilson's creek. We children could never guess her age—she seemed ancient—and she always smelled of home-made lye soap and wild herbs. She came more often to the local birthings than the local doctor did. And in spring she brought a Sunshine Cake to share with our family.

1¾ cups sifted cake flour
4 eggs, separated
3 tablespoons cold water
1½ cups sugar
1 teaspoon salt

1 teaspoon lemon juice, strained
½ cup boiling water
½ teaspoon cream of tartar
A Simple Old-fashioned Lemon
Sauce (recipe follows), optional

Preheat oven to 325°F. Set out a 9-inch tube pan. Measure flour and set aside until needed. In a large mixing bowl, beat *4 egg yolks* with cold water until they are foamy. Add sugar and beat until a light creamy yellow. Add salt, lemon juice, and boiling water. Stir together until well blended. Turn flour all at once into egg mixture and beat until a smooth batter is formed. Using a rotary or electric beater, beat the *4 egg whites* and cream of tartar into stiff peaks. Carefully, so as not to reduce the volume of the egg whites, fold egg whites into batter. Gently spoon batter into the tube pan. Bake until light golden brown, about 1 hour, then insert a toothpick into the center of the top of the cake; if it comes out clean the cake is done.

Remove the cake from the oven. Turn the cake upside down on a wire rack and let cool in the pan. When thoroughly cooled, using a knife blade or spatula, loosen the cake from the pan and turn it out onto a cake plate. Serve unfrosted or spoon A Simple Old-fashioned Lemon Sauce over it.

$\mathscr{A}$ SIMPLE OLD-FASHIONED LEMON SAUCE

makes 1½ cups lemon sauce

½ cup sugar
1 tablespoon cornstarch
⅛ teaspoon salt
1 cup boiling water

2 tablespoons butter or margarine
2 tablespoons lemon juice, strained
Grated rind of 1 lemon
1 egg yolk, beaten

In the top of a double boiler, combine sugar, cornstarch, and salt. Pour boiling water slowly over dry ingredients, stirring constantly. Over medium heat, cook 5 minutes. Remove from heat and add butter, lemon juice, and grated lemon rind. Remove from heat. Pour ½ *cup* of the hot lemon sauce over egg yolk, stirring to blend; return egg mixture to the *remaining* sauce. Return to heat and cook 1 minute more. Remove from heat and turn into a bowl; cool.

NOTE: Recipe may be doubled if you need more sauce for another use. It's delicious over plain cakes, gingerbread, or puddings.

THE COUNTRY MOTHERS COOKBOOK

OL' MISSUS UPJOHN'S DAFFODIL CAKE WITH SWEETENED WHIPPED CREAM

makes one 10-inch tube cake

IN THE OLD DAYS, as soon as the neighbors and relatives learned that a woman was in labor, they would begin to cook and bake. Almost before the baby was born, nearby folk would drop by for a minute to leave off a little something to eat. If the baby came in early spring when eggs were plentiful, more than one lady would send a lovely Daffodil Cake to grace the kitchen table, giving the occasion a festive touch.

YELLOW PART

¾ cup sifted cake flour
1 teaspoon baking powder
¼ teaspoon salt
6 egg yolks

¾ cup sugar
¼ cup boiling water
1 teaspoon lemon juice

Preheat oven to 350°F. Line a 10–inch tube pan with waxed paper, cutting a circle for the bottom and lining the side with a straight band.

TO MIX THE YELLOW PART

Sift flour with baking powder and salt. Beat yolks with sugar until they are thick and fluffy. Then alternately add flour and boiling water to yolk mixture, beating well after each addition. Add lemon juice and stir to blend. Set aside until white part is mixed.

WHITE PART

¾ cup sifted cake flour
½ teaspoon cream of tartar
¼ teaspoon salt

6 egg whites
¾ cup sugar
1 teaspoon vanilla extract

Sweetened Whipped Cream (recipe follows)

TO MIX THE WHITE PART

Sift flour with cream of tartar and salt. Beat egg whites until stiff; fold in sugar gently, 1 tablespoon at a time. Fold in flour and add vanilla, blending carefully so as not to reduce the volume of the beaten egg whites.

Using a large spoon, alternately drop yellow and white batter into the prepared tube pan. Bake at 350°F for 10 minutes, then turn the heat down to

300°F and bake for another 40 minutes. When the cake is golden brown on top, test for doneness by sticking a toothpick into the center top of the cake; if it comes out clean, the cake is done. Remove the pan from oven and turn upside down on a wire rack to cool. When thoroughly cool, remove the cake from the pan, loosening it around the edges if necessary with a knife blade or spatula. Turn out onto a cake plate. Serve without icing or frost the top with mounds of Sweetened Whipped Cream.

SWEETENED WHIPPED CREAM

makes 2⅓ cups

1 cup heavy cream   1 teaspoon vanilla extract
¼ cup sugar

Beat cream until well fluffed and begins to mound. Add sugar a little at a time, beating after each addition. Add vanilla and beat a few times to blend. Continue beating as necessary until cream is glossy. Serve in dollops on cake (or desserts). For thicker cream, beat a little longer, but pay close attention to the texture you are developing, stopping the beater now and then to pull it out of the cream. When thick, whipped cream is ready; the beater will come out leaving a pretty firm hole in the cream. Such cream is used as frosting or in pastry cases. When overwhipped, the cream will taste greasy.

CHOCOLATE ANGEL FOOD CAKE

makes one 10-inch tube cake

UNCLE BUD USED TO say, "When new babies come, mother-in-laws are a welcome sight." His mother-in-law usually made her famous Chocolate Angel Food Cake more than once during her stay, which endeared her to the children and to Uncle Bud.

10 egg whites
½ teaspoon salt
1 teaspoon cream of tartar
1½ cups sugar
¾ cup cake flour

¼ cup unsweetened powdered
    cocoa (no substitutes)
1 teaspoon vanilla extract
Sweetened Whipped Cream (page
    17), optional

Preheat oven to 350°F. Set out a 10-inch ungreased tube pan.

Beat egg whites with salt until frothy. Add cream of tartar and beat until stiff but not dry. Fold in sugar, 1 tablespoon at a time. Sift flour and cocoa together and add 1 tablespoon at a time. Fold vanilla into the batter. Pour into the tube pan and bake until firm to the touch, about 1 hour. Remove the pan from the oven and turn upside down on a wire rack to cool. When completely cool, take the cake gently out of the pan. Serve plain or frost with Sweetened Whipped Cream.

JANE WATSON HOPPING

$\mathcal{M}$AMA LOWERY'S OLD-FASHIONED TEA BISCUITS

makes about 3 dozen biscuits

THE LOWERYS HAD NINETEEN children of all ages and lived on a hardscrabble farm; even so, there seemed to be plenty of food and love to go around. Warm and generous people, they were the first to come to a birthing. Leading or riding on an old horse, they would bring a soft knitted shawl for the mother, a crocheted bonnet or a quilt for the baby, a brace of freshly skinned rabbits, and usually a basket of their mother's tea biscuits for the little ones.

4 cups sifted all-purpose flour
2 teaspoons baking powder
¼ teaspoon salt
1 tablespoon ground cinnamon
½ teaspoon ground ginger
½ teaspoon ground cloves
1 cup butter or margarine

1 cup firmly packed light brown
 sugar
4 eggs
1 cup milk
1 teaspoon vanilla extract
1 cup raisins
½ cup nut meats, optional

Preheat oven to 375°F. Set out a large cookie sheet.

Into a large bowl, sift flour with baking powder, salt, cinnamon, ginger, and cloves. With a pastry blender or hands, work butter into flour mixture. Add sugar and stir to blend (work lumps out with the fingers if needed). In a medium bowl, beat the eggs to a froth; add milk and vanilla and stir together. Make a well in the dry ingredients; pour in the liquid ingredients, all at once, and stir to blend. Add raisins (nuts, too, if desired) and fold into the dough.

Turn the dough out onto a well-floured surface. Knead, sprinkling on additional flour as needed, a dozen times to form a cohesive ball. Pat or roll out ½ inch thick; cut with a biscuit cutter. Lay rounds, not touching, on a cookie sheet and bake until well risen and browned, about 10 to 15 minutes, depending on the size of the biscuits. When stored in an airtight container, these sweet biscuits keep very well.

NOTE: If you don't like raisins, select another recipe; they are an important part of the sweetness and flavor in this biscuit.

JANE WATSON HOPPING

Just by the Garden Walk

WHEN SPRING BEGINS TO blossom, country women and girls leave their kitchens, take up shovels, rakes, and hoes, and work to beautify the homeplace. Old-fashioned flowers like purple and white flags (iris) need to be weeded, and white and deep-rose heliotrope beds need refurbishing. If rains come alternately with warm, balmy weather, the clover, alfalfa, and grasses outdo themselves until the whole farmstead is awash in a sea of green.

PANSIES

THE pansy blossoms please me so,
　　With faces all awry:
See this one looking at the earth,
　　And that one at the sky.

While this one laughs, that yonder frowns,
　　And here's one wants to talk;
And all this happens ev'ry day
　　Just by the garden walk.

—Thomas Tapper

THE COUNTRY MOTHERS COOKBOOK

I love all of the days
Of the beautiful world,
Every day every hour and minute.
I could go on living forever and never
Grow weary of any-thing in it.

O Little Babes of Mine

THERE IS NOTHING QUITE so lovely as the innocence of small children, who for a fragment of time have not been spoiled or touched by life. What joy to see their ability to love and be loved budding out; their confidence growing by leaps and bounds; the blossoming of that rare flower—true caring for others.

JANE WATSON HOPPING

SITHA JANE'S MUFFINS FOR BABIES

makes 12 medium muffins

THIS RECIPE MAKES VERY simple, delicious muffins that contain little sugar or fat, both of which Grandma thought were indigestible for her younger children.

2 cups, minus 2 rounded
    tablespoons all-purpose flour
2 teaspoons baking powder
½ teaspoon baking soda
Scant ½ teaspoon salt

2 tablespoons sugar
1 egg, lightly beaten
1 cup milk
2 tablespoons butter, melted

Preheat oven to 400°F. Grease muffin tin (12 cups).

Into a large bowl, sift flour, baking powder, soda, and salt. Add sugar and stir to blend. In a small bowl, combine egg, milk, and melted butter. Make a well in the dry ingredients. Pour liquid mixture into it. With a large-tined fork, stir the ingredients together just enough to dampen the flour mixture. Spoon into prepared muffin cups, about two-thirds full. Bake until golden brown, about 15 minutes. Remove from oven. Cool 5 to 8 minutes. Remove from pan and serve hot or cold.

A WINDY DAY

THE dawn was a dawn of splendor,
    And the blue of the morning skies
Was as placid and deep and tender
    As the blue of a baby's eyes;
The sunshine flooded the mountain,
    And flashed over land and sea
Like the spray of a glittering fountain. —
    But the wind—the wind—Ah me!

—James Whitcomb Riley

$\mathcal{A}$DA'S CORNSTARCH PUDDING (BLANCMANGE)

makes 4 to 6 servings

ADA LOVED THIS SIMPLE-TO-MAKE, nourishing pudding. She sweetened it so lightly that she could serve it even to her very small children. Sometimes she added one whole egg to the recipe.

1¾ cups cold skim milk, plus ¼ cup
    more for moistening cornstarch
3 tablespoons cornstarch

¼ cup sugar (less if desired)
⅛ teaspoon salt
1 teaspoon vanilla extract

Pour *1¾ cups cold milk* into the top of a double boiler; heat to scalding. In a small bowl, combine remaining *¼ cup milk* with cornstarch, sugar and salt; stir until smooth, then add all at once to hot milk, stirring to prevent lumping. Cover and cook an additional 3 to 4 minutes, stirring two or three times. When done, remove the top part of the double boiler and set pudding aside to cool. Add vanilla, stirring to blend. Turn pudding into an attractive bowl, or spoon it into individual serving dishes.

Effie teased her children gently; she thought it helped them develop a sense of humor. When they took it well, laughed and teased back, she knew they felt good about themselves inside.

A LITTLE GENTLEMAN

I know a well-bred little boy who never says "I can't";
He never says "Don't want to," or "You've got to," or "You sha'nt";
He never says "I'll tell mama!" or calls his playmates "mean."
A lad more careful of his speech I'm sure was never seen!

He's never ungrammatical—he never mentions "ain't";
A single word of slang from him would make his mother faint!
And now I'll tell you why it is (lest this should seem absurd):
He's now exactly six months old, and cannot speak a word!

—Hannah G. Fernald

JANE WATSON HOPPING

$\mathcal{E}$FFIE'S MINCED ROAST CHICKEN FOR LITTLE ONES

makes 1½ or more cups minced chicken and 1 quart thin gravy

IN THE OLD DAYS, as soon as children were able to eat solids, they sat at the table with the rest of the family, often on their mother's lap or father's knee. Gradually, as they grew older and had more teeth, bits of mashed or minced food were given to them. Effie thought a growing child needed a little finely mashed egg and minced meat, preferably chicken—roasted, not boiled, for flavor.

1 tender young frying chicken
½ teaspoon salt
1 medium carrot, peeled
1 stalk celery, washed, trimmed,
    and halved

1 quart cold water
No black pepper
3 tablespoons cornstarch

Preheat oven to 375°F. Set out a small covered roast pan or a large covered casserole.

Remove skin and all visible fat from chicken. Salt and place in the pan. Add carrot, celery, and water. Cover and cook in oven until meat falls off the bone, about 1½ hours. Remove chicken from pan and place, bones and all, in a colander; run hot water over meat to wash off any fat that coats it. Bone and mince both dark and light meat while still hot. Set aside to cool at room temperature, then refrigerate.

Remove carrot and celery from broth; discard. Set broth in a cool place until sediment settles to the bottom and fat rises to the surface. When cool, refrigerate until chilled. Skim off fat from the top of congealed broth. Reheat broth, strain if you wish to clarify further, and add enough water to make about 1 quart. Bring to a boil and thicken only slightly with about 3 tablespoons cornstarch moistened in cold water. When cool, refrigerate. Serve warmed chicken moistened with the gravy.

O Drowsy Winds, Awake, and Blow the Snowy Blossoms Back to Me

SPRINGTIME IN THE COUNTRY is a magical time. There is a tender newness about it, the colors are clear and awe-inspiring, the air so fresh it takes our breath away. Such promises of new birth invade the spirit, urging us to linger in the sunshine and let our minds wander and our senses reel.

Captured by the beauty of the season, we take the children outside to walk about, exploring the wonders that lie buried in the dewy grass—clover and myriads of other delicate herbs—until we come upon tiny blue and yellow flowers in full bloom, defying wind and weather. Or we stand among the little ones beneath an old apple tree and let the breezes shower us with snowy petals, marveling at the sky.

GRACE AT EVENING

FOR all the beauties of the day,
The innocence of childhood's play,
For health and strength and laughter sweet,
Dear Lord, our thanks we now repeat.

For this our daily gift of food
We offer now our gratitude,
For all the blessings we have known
Our debt of gratefulness we own.

Here at the table now we pray,
Keep us together down the way;
May this, our family circle, be
Held fast by love and unity.

Grant, when the shades of night shall fall,
Sweet be the dreams of one and all;
And when another day shall break
Unto Thy service may we wake.

—Edgar A. Guest

JANE WATSON HOPPING

Now I Lay Me Down to Sleep

GRANDMA MEEKINS INSISTED THAT all of the small children had to be in bed by dark. Each night as the shadows began to fall, the children lined up to wash the dirt off of their faces, hands and arms, feet and legs, while their grandmother reminded them that in their household they slept in clean beds. When they were in their nightclothes, she would go tuck them in and read or sing to them. They loved "Cradle Song," and why not, for she had sung it to them all while rocking them as babies.

THE COUNTRY MOTHERS COOKBOOK

Cloud-Light Lemon Sponge Pudding

makes 6 servings

GREAT–GRANDMA THOUGHT this was just right for a child's bedtime snack.

1 tablespoon all-purpose flour
1 cup sugar
Pinch salt (no more than
⅛ teaspoon)
2 eggs, separated, yolks beaten to
a froth, whites stiffly beaten

1 cup milk
Grated rind of 1 lemon
Juice of 1 lemon, strained
2 tablespoons butter or margarine,
melted, then cooled to
lukewarm

Preheat oven to 350°F. Set out a 1½- to 2-quart pudding dish.

Into a medium bowl, sift flour with sugar and salt. Blend in beaten egg yolk; add milk, grated lemon rind, and lemon juice; beat well. Then add melted butter and beat a few strokes more. Lastly fold in stiffly beaten egg whites. Turn into pudding dish and set into a pan of hot water (the water should reach one-third to one-half way up the sides of the mold).

Bake until sponge is lightly colored, custard is on the bottom and cake is on the top, about 45 minutes.

JANE WATSON HOPPING

The Patter of Little Feet

WHEN MY DAUGHTER COLLEEN was born, she weighed only four and a half pounds. For more than a year we had to watch her weight and feed her very carefully. My father came to visit and watched us taking care of this fragile baby. He thought she was quite special.

When he came to visit about three months later, he brought me the best blender he could find—money was no object—and he told me, "She'll grow better if you feed her real food and make it yourself."

She is twenty-seven now, a beautiful, healthy young woman, and if her grandfather could see her, he would mist up at the sight.

DRIED PEACH NUGGETS

makes about 3 dozen nuggets

IN OUR FAMILY, WE have always thought these little nuggets were a nice substitute for candy and felt comfortable letting small children eat them.

1 cup (6 ounces) dried peaches (see note)
⅓ cup unsweetened shredded coconut

1 tablespoon orange juice
3 tablespoons finely chopped almonds

Put peaches through the food grinder, using the fine blade. Add coconut and grind again. Stir in orange juice and mix well. Divide into 3 equal portions; wrap each portion separately and refrigerate to chill. When thoroughly chilled, work one portion at a time, rolling it back and forth on a smooth surface to form a narrow rope. Sprinkle with *1 tablespoon chopped almonds* and roll over nuts to coat the surface of the peach confection. Slice diagonally into 1½-inch slices. Continue with remaining 2 portions as instructed above.

NOTE: If peaches are not moist and chewy, place them in a wire strainer and steam them over boiling water for 5 minutes before grinding.

AUNT FANNY'S ARKANSAS BLACK APPLE COOKIES

makes about 4½ dozen cookies

ALONG ABOUT LATE MARCH or early April, most of the fall apples in the cellar or apple house began to spoil, but not the Arkansas Blacks, which remained hard through the cold weather and began to ripen only after Christmas. Aunt Fanny, taking advantage of this extended keeping quality, used them daily until they were all gone—much to the delight of the children.

½ cup butter or margarine
1½ cups firmly packed light brown
    sugar
1 egg
1 cup all-purpose flour
1 cup fine-ground whole-wheat flour
1 teaspoon baking soda
½ teaspoon salt
2 teaspoons ground cinnamon

½ teaspoon freshly grated nutmeg
¼ teaspoon ground cloves
⅓ cup apple cider
⅓ cup peeled, cored, and finely
    chopped apple (Jonathan,
    Red Delicious, Winesap, or
    Spitzenberg apples may be
    used)
1 cup golden raisins

Preheat oven to 400°F. Thoroughly grease a large baking sheet.

In a large bowl, cream butter and sugar together until light. Beat in egg. Sift flours with soda, salt, cinnamon, nutmeg, and cloves into a medium bowl. Add flour mixture to butter mixture alternately with cider. Fold in chopped apple and raisins. Drop by heaping teaspoonfuls onto the prepared baking sheet.

Bake until lightly browned, 10 to 12 minutes. Remove pan from oven, transfer cookies to brown paper. When completely cooled, store in a container that allows some air circulation.

JANE WATSON HOPPING

*I*NGER'S NORWEGIAN KRINGLE

makes about 4 dozen cookies

IT WAS A FINE day when Mother's friend Inger came visiting with a plate of these simple but good cookies. Mother thought they were akin to some Welsh tea cakes she liked. Inger's cookies were always plain without icing; we liked ours lightly covered with Fudge Glaze (page 32).

1 cup sugar
1 cup dairy sour cream
⅓ cup hot water
¼ cup unsweetened powdered
   cocoa
3 cups all-purpose flour

2 teaspoons ground cinnamon
1 teaspoon salt
¾ teaspoon baking soda
Simple Powdered Sugar Glaze
   (recipe follows)

Preheat oven to 350°F. Grease a large baking sheet.

    Combine sugar and sour cream in a large bowl, stirring until sugar is dissolved. Pour hot water over cocoa and stir into a paste; blend into the sugar mixture. Sift flour with salt, cinnamon, and soda into a medium bowl. Add flour mixture all at once to sugar mixture and stir together. Drop by teaspoonfuls onto the prepared baking sheet. Bake until firm to the touch, 15 to 18 minutes. Remove from oven and transfer to brown paper. While still warm, dip into A Simple Powdered Sugar Glaze. Let cookies cool completely and the glaze set before serving. The cookies will keep for a day or two in a container with a lid that allows a little air circulation; for longer storage freeze.

𝒜 SIMPLE POWDERED-SUGAR GLAZE

makes about ⅔ cup

1 cup powdered sugar
1 tablespoon milk

1 teaspoon vanilla extract

Mix sugar with milk and vanilla, beating until smooth. Immediately brush or dribble over tops of cookies, or dip tops lightly in the glaze, then turn right side up and place on brown paper to let the glaze set.

𝒥UDGE GLAZE

makes about ⅔ cup

5 tablespoons butter
¼ cup milk
About 1 to 2 tablespoons boiling
    water

¼ cup plus 2 tablespoons
    unsweetened cocoa powder
1 teaspoon vanilla extract
1 cup powdered sugar

In the top of a double boiler, combine the butter and milk and cook just until butter melts and milk is hot. Remove from heat. Stir just enough boiling water into the cocoa to make a paste. Add cocoa paste to the butter mixture and stir to blend. Stir in vanilla and then sugar. If the glaze is too thick, add a little more hot water.

THE SPIRIT OF THE HOME

DISHES to wash and clothes to mend,
    And always another meal to plan,
Never the tasks of a mother end
    And oh, so early her day began!
Floors to sweep and the pies to bake,
    And chairs to dust and the beds to make.

Oh, the home is fair when you come at night
    And the meal is good and the children gay,
And the kettle sings in its glad delight
    And the mother smiles in her gentle way;
So great her love that you seldom see
Or catch a hint of the drudgery.

Home, you say, when the day is done,
    Home to comfort and peace and rest;
Home where the children romp and run—
    There is the place that you love the best!
Yet what would the home be like if you
Had all of its endless tasks to do?

Would it be home if she were not there,
    Brave and gentle and fond and true?
Could you so fragrant a meal prepare?
    Could you the numberless duties do?
What were the home that you love so much,
Lacking her presence and gracious touch?

She is the spirit of all that's fair;
    She is the home you think you build;
She is the beauty you dream of there;
    She is the laughter with which it's filled—
She, with her love and her gentle smile,
Is all that maketh the home worth while.

—Edgar A. Guest

Aunt Mabel and Uncle Arch

JANE WATSON HOPPING

Old-fashioned Country Mothers

ALL OF THE WOMEN in our old-time families, Effie more than any other, tended to believe that God had endowed them with strength, mental and physical, and expected them to use both. Effie would tell all of us girls that no one amounts to anything unless they have enough backbone to stand up for what they believe to be right. And she would add, "That means girls as well as boys."

Effie, like her mother and grandmother before her, worked hard on the farm, doing man's work as well as the myriad things a country mother does for home and family. She was a practical visionary. She could see a rocky, weed-filled field as an opportunity to grow herbs that could be sold in town, or insist that it was practical to raise sheep with black or brown wool as well as white, because dark wool, once spun and mixed with the white, could be made into lovely rugs that she could keep or sell.

Family-Size Recipes

MOST OLD–TIME FAMILIES HAD personal recipes that the women had worked up to make enough to feed a family of ten, twelve, or counting grandparents and perhaps a maiden aunt or bachelor uncle or even hired hands (all living in the home or on the farm), sixteen or more.

Our friend Jake, a great bear of a man, the eldest of thirteen children, fondly remembers baking day at home when his mother and sisters made dozens of cookies, a huge sheet cake, more than one kind of bread, and at least four pies. He was a big, gangling, hungry boy whose mother often saved back a whole loaf of her fragrant hot bread for him, which he would break open with his hands, spread thickly with butter, and wash down with a quart or more of icy cold milk.

COLLEEN'S FAVORITE SUGAR COOKIES

makes 6 dozen or more cookies

WHEN OUR DAUGHTER COLLEEN was about eight, we practiced until we got this family-size recipe just right. The dough can be made into balls and pressed down with a fork; or it can be shaped into rolls, chilled, and then cut into ¼-inch slices. As it is most often made at our house, it can also be rolled into holiday cookies, using a cookie cutter that leaves an imprinted design on top of the cookie.

2 cups butter or margarine
    (1 pound)
2 cups sugar
4 eggs, beaten until frothy
1 teaspoon vanilla extract

1 teaspoon salt
5 cups sifted all-purpose flour
Simple Powdered-Sugar Glaze
    (page 32)

Preheat oven to 400°F. Set out two large baking sheets.

In a large bowl, cream butter and sugar until light. Add eggs, vanilla, and salt, stirring until well blended. Add the flour all at once, and stir until a cohesive dough is formed. Turn out on a lightly floured surface and knead only until dough can be handled. Divide into 3 portions; wrap 2 portions in waxed paper and refrigerate until needed. Roll the remaining third of the dough ¼-inch thick. Cut with fancy cookie cutters. Place cookies about 1 inch apart on the baking sheet. Bake until lightly colored around the edges, 10 to 12 minutes (don't overbake).

Meanwhile prepare the second batch of dough for baking, filling the second baking sheet with raw cookies. When the first batch is done, remove from oven and put in the second pan to bake. Immediately transfer baked cookies to brown paper to cool. Repeat entire process with the final portion of dough. Decorate cooled cookies, if you wish, using A Simple Powdered-Sugar Glaze, tinted with food coloring or left plain.

*R*ANDY'S WALNUT OATMEAL COOKIES

makes 7 to 8 dozen cookies

THIS RECIPE, ONLY THIRTY years old, is one that I worked up for our son Randy and his friends. The dough is heavy, and he or one of the other boys usually stirred it for me while I added the ingredients.

2 cups butter or margarine
   (1 pound)
2⅓ cups light brown sugar
   (1 pound)
4 eggs, lightly beaten
2 teaspoons vanilla extract
4 cups all-purpose flour

1 teaspoon baking soda
2 teaspoons salt
4 cups dry quick-cooking oats
1½ cups walnuts, chopped,
   optional
1½ cups chocolate chips, optional

Preheat oven to 400°F. Set out two large baking sheets.

In a very large bowl, using a pastry blender, cut butter into sugar until blended; don't overblend (bits of butter may be seen in the sugar). Add eggs and vanilla, and stir vigorously. Sift flour with soda and salt. Turn all at once into the butter mixture and stir to form a soft dough. Add oats, nuts and chocolate chips. Stir together.

Drop by teaspoonfuls onto the baking sheets, pressing down with fork or fingertips. Bake until golden brown and firm to the touch, about 10 to 12 minutes. Remove pans from oven and transfer cookies to brown paper for cooling. Store in airtight containers or freeze (will keep frozen for a month or more).

VARIATION: To make Peanut Butter Oatmeal Cookies, reduce butter to 1½ cups, add ⅔ cup crunchy peanut butter, and substitute ½ cup peanuts for walnuts.

DAD'S CREAM SHEET CAKE

makes 18 to 20 servings

THIS OLD-FASHIONED CAKE CONTAINS less sugar and fat than one might think. Country women knew how to judge the percentage of butterfat that was apt to be in the cream they planned to cook with. One cup of heavy cream had about 50 percent butterfat (½ cup butterfat and ½ cup milk), light cream 33 percent (⅓ cup butterfat and ⅔ cup milk). With this educated guess, they knew how much milk would be required for a cake (proportions being the same for most butter cakes—½ cup fat to 1 cup milk).

This cake can be served with or without frosting. Without frosting, the flavor and texture of the cake make it nice for use in fruit shortcakes, which old-time people topped with heavy cream or whipped cream.

2 cups heavy cream
1 cup skim milk
4 large eggs, beaten to a froth
2 teaspoons vanilla extract
1 teaspoon lemon extract or about
   2 tablespoons lemon juice

1⅔ cup sugar
4½ cups sifted all-purpose flour
2 teaspoons baking powder
1 teaspoon baking soda
1 teaspoon salt

Preheat oven to 375°F. Grease bottom of a 10½ × 15½ × 1–inch jelly-roll pan.

In a medium bowl, combine cream, milk, and eggs. Add vanilla and lemon extracts, stirring to blend. Add sugar, beating just enough to blend into the cream mixture. In a very large bowl, sift flour with baking powder, soda, and salt. Making a well in the flour mixture, gradually stir in cream mixture. Beat lightly until a smooth batter is formed, then turn into the prepared pan. Using a spatula, spread dough evenly into the corners of the pan.

Bake until golden brown around the edges and light golden brown on top, 35 to 40 minutes. Remove pan from oven; let cake cool in the pan. Leftover cake may be cut into pieces, wrapped, and frozen for later use. When needed for use, leave wrapper on cake and thaw at room temperature.

GRANDMA KING'S PATTY-PAN BREAD

makes 24 rolls

THIS OLD-FASHIONED BUSY-DAY RECIPE goes well with stew or beans simmered on the back of a woodstove (or in a Crockpot). We love it because it is quick to make, rises only once in the pan, and requires little clean-up. And it is delicious eaten plain without butter or jam.

3 packages granulated yeast
1 cup cream
1 cup boiling water
½ cup sugar

2 teaspoons salt
4 cups all-purpose flour, plus about
   1 cup more

Preheat oven to 425°F. Thoroughly grease a 10½ × 15½ × 1-inch jelly-roll pan. Set aside until needed.

Into a large mixing bowl, put yeast. Combine cream and boiling water and cool to lukewarm (105°F to 115°F); pour over yeast. Add sugar and salt. Let set for about 10 minutes. Then turn *4 cups flour* all at once into yeast mixture. Stir until a soft batterlike dough is formed. Add as much of the remaining *1 cup flour* as is needed to make a very soft dough, one that can be easily handled. Turn into the prepared pan and, after dusting the hands with flour, pat dough evenly over the pan.

Using a sharp knife, cut the dough lengthwise into 3 ribbons, then crosswise 8 times to mark off 24 rolls. Set in a warm place until risen, about 45 minutes. In cool weather, I set my rolls over the oven for quick rising.

Bake until well puffed and golden brown, 30 to 35 minutes. To test for doneness, check bottom of rolls, which should be a rich golden brown. Remove from oven. Serve piping hot, or cool in the pan. To reheat, cut off as many rolls as are needed, wrap in foil, and warm in a hot oven for 20 to 25 minutes. To freeze, wrap in foil, and then put in large freezer bag and fasten shut. Will keep frozen for about two months.

$\mathcal{A}$ CROWD-PLEASING APPLE DESSERT

makes 12 to 15 servings

OUR PARENTS, MOTHER'S SISTERS and brothers, grandpa, and cousins had get-togethers nearly every week to share birthdays, special events, or children's successes. This easy-to-make apple dish topped off many of those family pot-luck suppers.

Sweet Pastry Crust (recipe follows)
8 cups (about 8 large) peeled,
    cored, and sliced apples
    (Jonathan or Golden Delicious,
    as preferred)

1½ cups sugar
1 tablespoon ground cinnamon
1 egg, slightly beaten

Make crust and refrigerate before preparing apple filling. Preheat oven to 375°F. Set out a 15½ × 10½ × 1-inch jelly-roll pan.

Combine apples with sugar and cinnamon and toss lightly. Divide chilled dough into 2 parts. On a lightly floured surface, roll one part into a rectangle slightly larger than the jelly-roll pan. Loosely fold dough into quarters, transfer to the pan, and open out. Adjust dough in the pan; arrange apples in an even layer. Roll out remaining dough, fold, lay over top of apples, and unfold. Moisten edges of bottom crust, press lightly together with top edges, and flute. Cut slits in the top crust to allow steam to escape. Brush crust with egg and sprinkle *3 tablespoons sugar* over the top.

Bake in hot oven 25 minutes; reduce heat to 350°F and bake until apples are done and crust is golden brown, about 15 minutes more. Remove from oven, cool in the pan on a wire rack. Serve while slightly warm in squares, topped with vanilla ice cream, if wished.

JANE WATSON HOPPING

*S*WEET PASTRY CRUST

makes enough pastry for one double-crust 15½ × 10½ × 1-inch dessert

3¾ cups all-purpose flour
¼ cup sugar plus 3 tablespoons for
    sprinkling over crust
½ teaspoon salt

1½ cups cold margarine
⅓ cup cold water, or slightly more
    if needed

Combine flour, *¼ cup sugar,* and salt. With a pastry blender, cut in margarine until particles are the size of peas. Sprinkle with *¼ cup cold water,* adding more as needed to gather dough into a ball. Refrigerate until apple filling is prepared, 15 to 20 minutes.

UNCLE SIDNEY'S LOGIC

PA wunst he scold' an' says to me,—
    "Don't *play* so much, but try
To *study* more, and nen you'll be
    A great man, by an' by."
Nen Uncle Sidney says, "You let
    Him *be* a boy an' play.—
The greatest man on earth, I bet,
    'Ud trade with him to-day!"

        —James Whitcomb Riley

A BAREFOOT BOY

A barefoot boy! I marked him at his play—
    For May is here once more, and so is he,—
    His dusty trousers, rolled half to the knee,
And his bare ankles grimy, too, as they:
Cross-hatchings of the nettle, in array
    Of feverish stripes, hint vividly to me
    Of woody pathways winding endlessly
Along the creek, where even yesterday
He plunged his shrinking body—gasped and shook—
    Yet called the water "warm," with never lack
Of joy. And so, half enviously I look
    Upon this graceless barefoot and his track,—
    His toe stubbed—ay, his big toe-nail knocked back
Like unto the clasp of an old pocketbook.

                  —James Whitcomb Riley

JANE WATSON HOPPING

When He Grows Up to Be a Man

VERA KAMPING'S BROTHERS, WAYNE and Wendell, and their cousin Gilbert—who from age sixteen and a half months to manhood was raised by Vera's parents—were lively as country boys can be. In spring, they gamboled over the countryside; in summer, they swam in the river, bodies flashing like silver-sided fish in the shade-speckled water; in winter, they glided over the ice with a grace no one expected from gangling farm boys.

Those were the days of knickers and passed-down clothes, of torn pants and shirts. Mothers were kept busy recycling all the garments that came into their hands, passing shirts and dresses down from older children to younger ones who could wear them. Those that didn't fit, or that were worn but still contained considerable good cloth, were remodeled. Vera remembers a man's suit that was practically new, both coat and pants, being given to her mother, who cut them down for one of the boys to wear to school.

THE COUNTRY MOTHERS COOKBOOK

RAYMOND'S BANANA-NANA-NANA PUDDING

makes 8 servings

DURING THE GREAT DEPRESSION my husband's father and his uncle moved back onto the family farm, where they grew vegetables for sale and developed a door-to-door produce route, thus creating jobs for themselves. When they began to make money, they bought off-farm items like bananas and sold them, too.

Raymond, my husband, remembers being four years old and waiting for the produce truck to return home. All he could think of were the bananas that might be left over. When the truck hove into sight, he would run out to greet his father or uncle and, jumping up and down, in a piping little voice yell, "I want a banana-nana-nana!" which after a bit of teasing his father or uncle would give him. And if there were several left, his mama would make him a banana-nana-nana pudding topped with crushed vanilla wafers or Sweetened Whipped Cream.

Lemon Cornstarch Pudding (recipe follows)
Vanilla wafers (about ⅓ of a one-pound box for lining serving dish, plus ½ cup crumbled wafers for topping pudding

6 large bananas
Sweetened Whipped Cream, optional topping (page 17)

Make Lemon Cornstarch Pudding. Set aside to cool. When at room temperature, assemble pudding.

Line a large attractive bowl with vanilla wafers, both the sides and the bottom. Alternately layer banana slices with Lemon Cornstarch Pudding. Top with wafer crumbs or with Sweetened Whipped Cream.

$\mathcal{L}$EMON CORNSTARCH PUDDING

makes about 6 servings

3 tablespoons cornstarch
1 cup sugar
¼ teaspoon salt
1 cup boiling water

2 cups milk
2 eggs, beaten
¼ teaspoon lemon extract
¼ teaspoon vanilla extract

Into the top of a double boiler, sift cornstarch, sugar, and salt. Gradually add boiling water, stirring constantly. Boil over direct heat until thickened, stirring constantly. Place the top of the double boiler over its base, making sure that boiling water in the base does not touch the bottom of the top pan. Add milk to cornstarch mixture, then eggs. Cook until thickened, about 15 minutes, stirring occasionally. Remove top from base, set aside to cool slightly, then add flavoring. Cool to room temperature.

$\mathcal{A}$UNT FANNY'S FOUR-CUP PUDDING

makes about 8 servings unless there are several boys in the family; then it serves 3

DURING THE LATE THIRTIES this was a popular dessert in our family. The tight times seemed to have eased a bit and the womenfolk could afford to try new things, to buy a can of pineapple and some marshmallows for such treats as this Four-Cup Pudding.

1 cup cold cooked rice
1 cup canned crushed pineapple,
    drained
1 cup quartered or small
    marshmallows

1 cup blanched almonds or walnuts,
    chopped
Sweetened Whipped Cream
    (page 17)

In a large bowl, combine rice, pineapple, marshmallows, and almonds. Chill thoroughly and serve in sherbet glasses, topped with Sweetened Whipped Cream.

THE ROUGH LITTLE RASCAL

A smudge on his nose and a smear on his cheek
And knees that might not have been washed in a week;
A bump on his forehead, a scar on his lip,
A relic of many a tumble and trip:
A rough little, tough little rascal, but sweet,
Is he that each evening I'm eager to meet.

A brow that is beady with jewels of sweat;
A face that's as black as a visage can get;
A suit that at noon was a garment of white,
Now one that his mother declares is a fright:
A fun-loving, sun-loving rascal, and fine,
Is he that comes placing his black fist in mine.

A crop of brown hair that is tousled and tossed;
A waist from which two of the buttons are lost;
A smile that shines out through the dirt and the grime,
And eyes that are flashing delight all the time:
All these are the joys that I'm eager to meet
And look for the moment I get to my street.

—Edgar A. Guest

The Fire Is 'Neath the Kettle

EDGAR A. GUEST, A poet loved by millions of Americans in the first quarter of this century, wrote about the things nearest and dearest to the human heart, and thus kept bright everyday folks' faith in that which is worthwhile.

His writings inspired common people to keep the home fires burning; to respect motherhood and family values; to have sympathetic understanding of children and insight into the fellowship of man; to have compassion for the problems of the toilers and the burdens of the downtrodden; and to treasure the natural beauty of plant and animal kingdoms and the grandeur of nature as a whole.

THE COUNTRY MOTHERS COOKBOOK

47

The Old-Time Family

UNCLE BUD FONDLY RECALLS memories of his childhood in the backwoods, and of the small house his father built for them out of logs. When his boy John was about seven years old, Uncle Bud taught him to recite this bit of poetry written by Edgar A. Guest:

From THE OLD-TIME FAMILY

WE were eight around the table in those happy days back then.
Eight that cleaned our plates of pot-pie and then passed them up again;
Eight that needed shoes and stockings, eight to wash and put to bed,
And with mighty little money in the purse, as I have said,
But with all the care we brought them, and through all the days of stress,
I never heard my father or my mother wish for less.

—Edgar A. Guest

JANE WATSON HOPPING

Home-cured Ham Baked in Milk

makes 6 servings

WHEN MAMA LOWERY HAD spring company, she fixed huge panfuls of this delicious ham, enough for her own large family and numerous guests. She baked an ovenful of new red potatoes, cooked a potful of Auntie's Garden-Fresh Peas and Baby Onions (page 50), and usually baked several Good Ol' Apple Pies with Tip-top Pastry Dough (page 52).

Center slice of ham, 2 inches thick
1 teaspoon dry mustard
¼ cup firmly packed light brown
    sugar

1 cup milk, or enough to barely
    cover ham

Preheat oven to 300°F. Grease a large flat casserole.

    Mix mustard and sugar together; spread over ham. Place meat in the casserole and add enough milk to cover. Bake until milk has reduced in volume and ham has browned lightly, 45 minutes to 1 hour. Remove from oven and serve immediately.

AUNTIE'S GARDEN-FRESH PEAS AND BABY ONIONS

makes 6 servings

OUR GRANDFATHER TAUGHT US how to judge whether or not peas were just right for picking. From him we learned to look for those that were encased in shiny green pods and to discard those filled to bursting, which were too mature and apt to taste mealy because the natural sugar had started to convert to starch. He also insisted that we throw out faded or discolored pods, which, he said, were defective or old. Fresh peas picked by Grandpa always tasted delicious.

2 cups freshly shelled peas (press
    the pod open with the thumbs
    and remove the peas)
1 cup small white onions
2 tablespoons butter or margarine

¼ teaspoon salt, plus a little more
    to adjust seasoning
Black pepper to taste
1 tablespoon minced parsley

Simmer peas and onions in separate saucepans with about 2 inches of lightly salted boiling water until each becomes tender, 10 to 20 minutes. Drain and combine in a large serving bowl; dress with butter, salt, pepper, and parsley. (Fresh basil may be substituted for parsley if the leaves are very small and tender.)

BERTIE'S YOUNG TURNIPS WITH BACON

makes 6 servings

BERTIE LOVED TENDER YOUNG turnips, so when we had them in the garden, we took her bunches now and again. She served peeled raw turnip slices when she did not have radishes and garnished a relish or meat tray with them. Sometimes she cut thin slices from a large mild turnip. Using a small cookie cutter, she then cut them into decorative designs. We loved her turnips with bacon.

12 young turnips

8 strips of bacon

JANE WATSON HOPPING

Wash, peel, and remove the tops from young turnips that are only 1½ to 2 inches in diameter, allowing 2 per serving. Cook the root in one pot and the greens in another until they are each tender-crisp. Chop the greens and lay them as a bed for the young turnips. Cook strips of bacon until crisp and crumble over the hot turnips. Salt and pepper to taste and serve.

$\mathcal{E}$ASY-TO-MAKE CORN MUFFINS

makes 1 dozen medium muffins

WHEN MOTHER FIXED A weekday supper of beans, baked potatoes, crisp-fried country bacon, and wilted greens, Grandpa thought the meal was incomplete unless she whipped up some corn muffins or corn bread, too.

1 cup sifted all-purpose flour
¾ cup yellow cornmeal
4 teaspoons baking powder
3 tablespoons sugar
¾ teaspoon salt

1 egg, well-beaten
1 cup milk
3 tablespoons butter or margarine, melted

Preheat oven to 400°F. Grease a 12-cup medium-size muffin tin.

Into a large bowl, sift flour with cornmeal, baking powder, sugar, and salt. In a small bowl, combine egg, milk, and melted butter, stirring to blend. Pour mixture into flour mixture and stir with a fork just enough to moisten dry ingredients (do not beat). Fill prepared muffin cups ⅔ full. Bake until muffins are golden brown, well risen, and firm to the touch, about 20 minutes. Serve piping hot.

GOOD OL' APPLE PIE WITH TIP-TOP PASTRY DOUGH

makes one 9-inch pie

THIS IS A VERY simple pattern for making pies. Grandma used to make them six at a time. We still make them in season by the dozens and freeze them uncooked or baked for winter use.

Tip-top Pastry Dough (recipe
    follows)
⅔ cup sugar
⅛ teaspoon salt
¾ teaspoon ground cinnamon
¼ teaspoon freshly grated nutmeg

5 cups peeled, cored and thinly
    sliced tart apples (Winesap,
    Arkansas Blacks, Northern Spy,
    and Jonathan or your favorite
    pie apple)
Butter, optional

Before peeling apples and making filling, prepare Tip-top Pastry Dough and refrigerate to chill. Preheat oven to 450°F.

In a small bowl, mix sugar, salt, and spices together; add *half* sugar mixture to the apples. (If apples lack tartness, add *2 tablespoons lemon juice*.)

On a lightly floured surface, roll out half of the chilled dough to ⅛ inch thickness. Loosely line a 9-inch pie pan (don't stretch the dough). Trim pastry even with the edge of the pan. Next, roll the other half of the dough ⅛ inch thick, fold in half, and cut several slits across the fold (to allow steam to escape during baking).

Sprinkle the *remaining half* of sugar mixture over bottom crust in the pan. Turn apple mixture into the pan and dot with butter, if wished. Moisten the edge of the bottom crust and adjust the folded crust over half the filling, opening out the crust and drawing it carefully across the entire top. Trim off surplus pastry with a knife; flute rim with thumb and forefinger to press crusts together. Bake until filling is done and crust is golden brown, about 50 minutes. Serve at room temperature or cold.

ᎢIP-TOP PASTRY DOUGH

makes enough dough for one 9-inch double-crust pie

1½ cups all-purpose flour, plus
    flour for rolling out dough
1 teaspoon baking powder
½ teaspoon salt

½ cup butter or margarine
1 teaspoon lemon juice
2 tablespoons cold water, or more
    if needed

Into a large bowl, sift flour, baking powder, and salt. With fingertips, rub butter into the flour mixture until the particles are about the size of a grain of rice. Refrigerate 2 hours, then set aside *½ cup* of the mixture. Add lemon juice and just enough cold water (add it about 1 tablespoon at a time) to make a stiff dough. Turn dough onto a floured surface. Knead lightly and roll into a rectangle about ¼ inch thick. Next, sprinkle the rolled pastry with *about ¼ cup of the reserved flour mixture*. Fold dough as you would a letter to make 3 layers. Turn the dough half way around, then roll again into a rectangle. Sprinkle on the *remaining ¼ cup flour mixture* and fold in thirds again. Roll and fold twice more. Divide dough into two equal portions. Refrigerate to chill.

THE COUNTRY MOTHERS COOKBOOK

The Lanes of Memory

ADOWN the lanes of memory bloom all the flowers of yesteryear,
And looking back we smile to see life's bright red roses reappear,
The little sprigs of mignonette that smiled upon us as we passed,
The pansy and the violet, too sweet, we thought those days, to last.

The gentle mother by the door caresses still her lilac blooms,
And as we wander back once more we seem to smell the old perfumes,
We seem to live again the joys that once were ours so long ago
When we were little girls and boys, with all the charms we used to know.

But living things grow old and fade; the dead in memory remain,
In all their splendid youth arrayed, exempt from suffering and pain;
The little babe God called away, so many, many years ago,
Is still a little babe to-day, and I am glad that this is so.

Time has not changed the joys we knew; the summer rains or winter snows
Have failed to harm the wondrous hue of any dew-kissed bygone rose;
In memory 'tis still as fair as when we plucked it for our own,
And we can see it blooming there, if anything, more lovely grown.

Adown the lanes of memory bloom all the joys of yesteryear,
And God has given you and me the power to make them reappear;
For we can settle back at night and live again the joys we knew
And taste once more the old delight of days when all our skies were blue.

—Edgar A. Guest

JANE WATSON HOPPING

Granny's Sweet Song

EFFIE, LIKE HER GRANDMOTHERS before her, is the silver thread that binds all of the younger generation to those of the past. Through her memories, continuity flows. She is the vessel in which the ancient family values reside.

Her grandchildren, nieces, and nephews all treasure the gifts of living she has given them, but most of all they hold close visions of Effie singing lullabies, and they recall sitting at her knee learning this soft and lilting song of long ago, which Effie, as a child, had learned from her own granny:

BENDEMEER'S STREAM

THERE'S a bower of roses by Bendemeer's stream,
And the nightingales sing round it all the day long;
In the time of my childhood 'twas like a sweet dream
To sit in the roses and hear the bird's song.

That bower and its music I ne'er shall forget,
But when alone in the bloom of the year—
I think, Is the nightingale singing there yet?
Are the roses still bright by the calm Bendemeer.

—Thomas Moore, Irish Folk Song

DAISY'S NUTMEG CAKE WITH LEMON CREAM-CHEESE FROSTING

WHEN DAISY WAS GROWING up, her Grandma Holt lived with them. She fondly remembers this little poem that her granny used to recite to her:

From FOR CHRISTMAS DAY

DON'T say she's lost her ribbon
    And her apron's all awry;
Don't speak of flour upon her nose
    And smut above her eye;
Don't tell her that the pans aren't greased;
    The powder's quite at fault,
That the heaping cup of sugar
    Was a heaping cup of salt;
Don't mention that the fire is out,
    'T would be a grave mistake—
Onlookers, keep your distance
    When Daisy's baking cake!

           —Nancy Byrd Turner

2 cups sifted cake flour
2½ teaspoons freshly grated
    nutmeg
1 teaspoon baking powder
½ teaspoon baking soda
¼ teaspoon salt
½ cup butter, softened at room
    temperature

1 teaspoon vanilla extract
1½ cups sugar
3 eggs, well beaten
1 cup buttermilk
Lemon Cream-Cheese Frosting
    (recipe follows)

Preheat oven to 350°F. Grease and lightly flour two round 9-inch layer-cake pans.

    Into a medium bowl, sift flour, nutmeg, baking powder, soda, and salt. In a large bowl, cream butter and vanilla together until butter is light. Add sugar gradually, creaming until fluffy after each addition. Add beaten eggs, one-third at a time, beating thoroughly after each addition.

Then alternately add flour mixture by fourths and milk by thirds to the creamed mixture, beating only until smooth after each addition. After the final portion of flour has been added, beat batter until smooth (don't overbeat).

Turn batter into prepared pans. Bake until cake is light golden brown and layers test done when pressed lightly with fingertips, about 30 minutes. Turn out on a wire rack to cool. When thoroughly cooled, frost. While old-fashioned cooks frosted this cake with a brown sugar seafoam frosting, we prefer this Lemon Cream-Cheese Frosting.

*L*EMON CREAM-CHEESE FROSTING

makes enough frosting to fill and frost tops and sides of one 9-inch two-layer cake

6 ounces cream cheese, softened at
   room temperature
1½ teaspoons lemon juice

½ teaspoon grated lemon peel
4 cups sifted powdered sugar

In a medium bowl, blend cream cheese, lemon juice, and peel. Add gradually, and blend in, powdered sugar. If frosting is too stiff to spread, blend in *1 teaspoon* cold water at a time until a light spreading consistency is obtained.

ADA'S TWO-COLORED COOKIES

makes about 5 dozen cookies

BLESSED WITH SIX GRANDCHILDREN who came over to see her quite frequently, Ada never tired of surprising them with something different. Her two-colored cookies astounded them all, so much so that they wanted to run down the country road to their friends' houses to share the delights, leaving the cookie jar empty again.

2 cups sifted cake flour
1 teaspoon baking powder
½ teaspoon salt
½ cup butter or margarine
⅔ cup sugar

1 egg
1 tablespoon milk
1 teaspoon vanilla extract
1 square unsweetened chocolate,
    melted

Into a large bowl, sift together flour, baking powder, and salt. In a second large bowl, cream butter, adding sugar gradually, then cream together until light. Add egg, milk, and vanilla; beat well. Then add the flour mixture, a small amount at a time, blending well after each addition.

Divide the dough into halves. To one half add chocolate; blend until dough is evenly colored. Shape chocolate and vanilla doughs into separate rolls, about 1½ to 2 inches in diameter. Lay together and twist to give marbled effect. Roll in waxed paper and chill overnight, or until firm enough to slice.

When dough is firm, preheat the oven to 375°F. Cut rolls into ¼-inch slices. Bake on ungreased baking sheet until light dough begins to brown, about 10 minutes.

JANE WATSON HOPPING

HIS MOTHER'S WAY

TOMPS 'ud allus haf to say
Somepin' 'bout "his mother's way."—
He lived hard-like—never jined
Any church of any kind.—
"It was Mother's way," says he,
"To be good enough fer *me*

And her too,—and certinly
 Lord has heerd *her* pray!"
Propped up on his dyin' bed,—
"Shore as Heaven 's overhead,
I'm a-goin' there," he said—
 "It was Mother's way."

—James Whitcomb Riley

GRANNY'S APPLE RAISIN COOKIES

makes 3 dozen cookies

APPLES WRINKLED BY WINTER storage, yet sweet as sugar, are perfect for these soft, chewy cookies.

1½ cups all-purpose flour
1 teaspoon baking powder
½ teaspoon soda
½ teaspoon salt
1 teaspoon ground cinnamon
¼ teaspoon freshly grated nutmeg
¾ cup butter or margarine,
    softened at room temperature
1 cup firmly packed light brown
    sugar

1 egg, unbeaten
1 tablespoon cold water
1 cup peeled, cored, and finely
    diced apple
1½ cups dry quick or old-fashioned
    oats
½ cup dark raisins

Preheat oven to 375°F. Grease a large baking sheet and set aside.

Into a large bowl, sift together flour, baking powder, soda, salt, cinnamon, and nutmeg. Add butter, sugar, egg, and water, beating until a smooth batter is formed, about 2 minutes. Fold in diced apple, rolled oats, and raisins. Drop by teaspoonfuls onto prepared baking sheet. (Roll dough in cinnamon sugar, if you wish.) Bake until well risen, golden brown, and firm to the touch, 12 to 15 minutes. Remove from oven, transfer to brown paper (an opened brown bag will do) to cool. When thoroughly cooled, store in an airtight container.

THE COUNTRY MOTHERS COOKBOOK

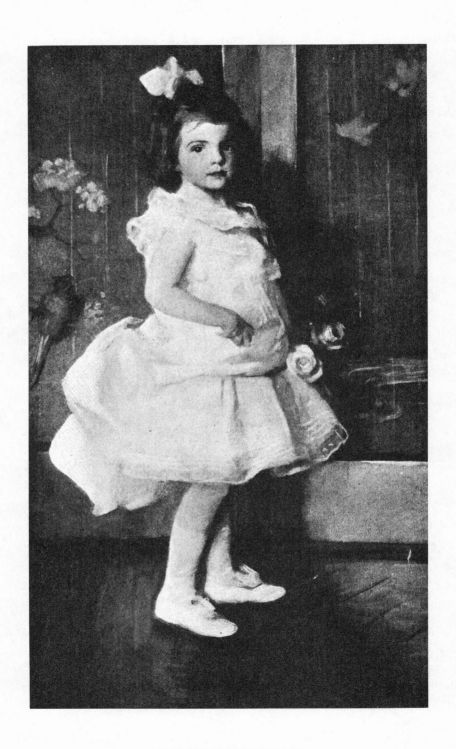

JANE WATSON HOPPING

An Easter Picnic and a Trip to Sutter's Mill

From IN FERVENT PRAISE OF PICNICS

PICNICS is fun 'at's purty hard to beat.
I purt' nigh ruther go to them than *eat.*—
I purt' nigh ruther go to them than go
With our Char*lot*ty to the Trick-Dog
Show!

—James Whitcomb Riley

By Easter, the weather was warm in California, just right for a picnic. And the perfect spot for such a joyful occasion was "the flat," which was the site of an old homestead in the hills near Coloma. All that was left was a meadow, a chimney, and a yellow rambler rose.

About ten in the morning, we would arrive to set up sawhorse tables over which sheets were thrown for tablecloths. And as the folks began to arrive, the food began to pile up. Boxes of carefully concealed colored eggs were put behind or under the table and we children were told to "leave things alone." Finally, there was an Easter egg hunt for a multitude of eggs (there had to be plenty, as Uncle Ben liked to hunt too), a great feast, and games—baseball, tag, kick-the-can, run-sheep-run, and others—until everyone was tired and until the table was cleaned up and the food put away.

Then, since Sutter's Mill was not very far away, there was a little trip for those who wanted to finish off the afternoon. The caravanning, probably instigated by Aunt Mabel, who tried to enrich our childhood experiences, did not take long. The site where gold was discovered in California in 1848 was no more than a shallow, rippling riverbed, but there was the hallowed feeling of history there. As we stood knee-deep in the icy water, carefully holding pie pans and learning from Aunt Mabel how to pan gold, the feeling of discovery was imminent.

$\mathscr{A}$DA'S EASTER SALAD

makes 6 servings

ADA'S BROTHER WALTER BUILT her a tight wooden box that had a compartment in the center which would hold her dishes of jellied salad or dessert, and all around it he left room for crushed ice with a little salt sprinkled over it. The box had a tight-fitting cover and holes drilled in the bottom to let melted ice water run out. All through the year she used her box to bring her favorite dishes to family potluck dinners and picnics, much to the delight of the children who loved everything Ada made.

2 envelopes unflavored gelatin
1 quart strained chicken broth from
    Boiled Chicken recipe
½ teaspoon salt
⅛ teaspoon black pepper
4 hard-cooked eggs, sliced
1 pimiento, cut into strips, for
    garnish

1 Boiled Chicken (recipe follows)
1 cup chopped Tomato Aspic (recipe
    follows)
2 sprigs parsley, for garnish
8 black olives, pitted and chopped
About ½ cup mayonnaise

Soften gelatin in *½ cup cold chicken broth* for 5 minutes. In a small saucepan, heat *remaining 3½ cups chicken broth* to boiling, adding salt and pepper (to taste). Add gelatin and stir until dissolved. Set aside until gelatin mixture begins to thicken. Then, glaze a chilled 1½-quart mold (pour about ⅔ cup jelly in the mold, then turn the mold about so that the jelly coats the sides). The jelly should be about 1½ inches thick in the bottom of the mold. Dip egg slices and pimiento pieces in liquid gelatin, place on bottom and sides of mold. Chill for about 15 minutes. Also set gelatin mixture to cool.

When gelatin has cooled to the consistency of egg whites, arrange sliced cooked chicken in the mold in alternate layers of light and dark meat. Fill the mold with *remaining* gelatin. Chill until firm.

Unmold salad onto a platter and serve garnished with chopped tomato aspic, parsley, and chopped black olives. Serve with a dollop of mayonnaise on top.

BOILED CHICKEN

2 quarts hot water
2 cups milk
3- to 5-pound chicken, left whole
2 teaspoons salt

1 teaspoon black pepper
2 stalks celery
1 small onion, peeled and quartered

In a large kettle, bring water and milk to a boil. (The milk tenderizes and whitens the meat.) Ease the chicken into the liquid; add salt, pepper, celery, and onion. Simmer slowly until meat is tender, 1 to 1½ hours, removing any scum that rises to the surface as chicken cooks. While cooking, keep chicken under the broth; if necessary, weight it down with a plate.

When chicken is done, transfer it to a casserole dish and set aside to cool. Leave broth in the kettle and set it to cool at room temperature until it is barely lukewarm; then refrigerate. Meanwhile, when chicken is cool enough to handle, remove skin and bones, and slice the meat; cover and set aside until needed. Strain cooled broth to make a clear stock, then measure out 1 quart. Add water as needed to make the quart.

TOMATO ASPIC

makes about 2 cups garnish

2 cups tomato juice
¼ cup chopped celery leaves
¼ cup minced green onions
1 tablespoon sugar
¾ teaspoon salt

1 envelope unflavored gelatin
¼ cup cold water
1 tablespoon lemon juice or cider
   vinegar

In a medium saucepan, heat tomato juice, celery leaves, onion, sugar, and salt. Simmer, covered, about 10 minutes. Meanwhile, in a small bowl, sprinkle gelatin evenly over cold water and let stand about 5 minutes to soften.

Lightly oil a small loaf pan (do not use olive oil or hardened fats). Remove tomato juice mixture from heat and strain into a 1-quart bowl. Immediately add softened gelatin to the tomato-juice mixture; stir until gelatin is completely dissolved. Pour mixture into the prepared loaf pan. Cool, then place in refrigerator to chill until firm. Just before using chop into small pieces.

SORGHUM-DIPPED SOUTHERN FRIED CHICKEN

makes 4 to 6 servings

AFTER THE FOLKS LEFT Missouri, Grandpa and Uncle Ben complained of never finding good sorghum; commercial syrup just didn't do justice to hot buttermilk biscuits, and it didn't taste right spooned over beans. The women complained, too, and tried one thing after another, hoping to find a good dip for their fried chicken. They never did improve on this delicious sorghum recipe.

1 cup all-purpose flour
1 teaspoon salt
½ teaspoon black pepper
1 teaspoon dried oregano leaves,
     pulverized

3-pound frying chicken, cut into
     serving pieces
½ cup light sorghum
Fat for frying, cooking oil if you
     wish

Preheat oven to 350°F.

In a small flat bowl, combine flour with salt, pepper, and oregano (to pulverize, roll between thumb and fingertips). Dip chicken pieces in sorghum (thinned slightly with water, if you like), and coat with flour mixture. Roll a second time in flour and set aside for 20 minutes. Put enough fat in a large heavy skillet to fill it ½ inch deep when melted. When fat is hot enough to brown a cube of bread in 1 minute, fry chicken, browning it on each side. Then place partially cooked chicken in a shallow baking pan and bake until tender, about 30 minutes. Serve hot or cold.

JANE WATSON HOPPING

$\mathcal{A}$UNT FANNY'S SILVER CAKE WITH FLUFFY WHITE FROSTING

makes one 9-inch two-layer cake

AUNTIE LOVED WHITE COOKIES, white bread, and this white cake with Fluffy White Frosting. And because it was so light and delicate, we girls thought it was something special, too.

3 cups sifted cake flour
3 teaspoons baking powder
½ teaspoon salt
½ cup butter or margarine,
    softened at room temperature
1 teaspoon vanilla extract

1½ cups sugar
1¼ cups milk
4 egg whites
Fluffy White Frosting (page 66)

Preheat oven to 375°F. Grease and dust with flour two round 9-inch layer-cake pans; set aside.

Into a medium bowl, sift flour, baking powder, and salt; sift together two more times. In a large bowl, cream butter until smooth. Then add vanilla and sugar gradually, creaming until light. To the butter-sugar mixture, alternately add flour mixture and milk; beat well after each addition.

In a medium bowl, beat egg whites into soft peaks. Then gently, so as not to lose volume, fold them into the batter. Turn into prepared pans.

Bake until light golden brown, firm to the touch, and a bit springy, about 25 to 30 minutes. Remove from oven, let set about 10 minutes, then turn out to cool on wire racks. When cool, frost with Fluffy White Frosting.

*F*LUFFY WHITE FROSTING

makes enough frosting to lightly fill and frost one 9-inch two-layer cake

2 tablespoons butter or margarine,
    softened at room temperature
2½ cups sifted powdered sugar
About 1 tablespoon milk

About 1 tablespoon heavy cream
¾ teaspoon lemon extract
⅛ teaspoon salt

In a medium bowl, cream butter; add ¾ *(almost 2 cups)* of sugar gradually, blending after each addition. Then, add the last of the sugar alternately with milk, then with cream until frosting has a light spreadable consistency. For a fluffy texture, beat well after each addition. Blend in lemon extract and salt.

*L*EMON-ORANGE FROSTING

makes enough to lightly fill and frost one 9-inch three-layer cake

4 tablespoons butter, softened at
    room temperature
3½ cups (1-pound box) powdered
    sugar
2 tablespoons fresh lemon juice,
    strained

¼ cup fresh orange juice, strained
    (more as needed)
2 teaspoons finely grated lemon
    peel
3 tablespoons finely grated orange
    peel

In a large bowl, cream butter, beating with a spoon until it is light and fluffy. Alternately, beginning with 1 cup of the powdered sugar, blend in sugar and combined lemon and orange juice, beating well after each addition. Last, beat in grated lemon and orange peel.

Mother's Gold Cake with Lemon-Orange Frosting

makes one 9-inch three-layer cake

OLD-TIME WOMEN LIKE MOTHER were playful cooks who used their skills to surprise and please those they loved, and to celebrate special occasions, such as our Easter trip to Sutter's Mill on the south fork of the American River.

The mill site became the birthplace of the California Gold Rush in 1848, when John A. Marshall picked up the first bright nugget while building a mill wheel for John A. Sutter's new sawmill.

¾ cup butter or margarine
1½ cups sugar
1 teaspoon lemon extract
8 egg yolks, well beaten
3 cups sifted cake flour

3 teaspoons baking powder
½ teaspoon salt
1 cup milk
Lemon-Orange Frosting (recipe opposite)

Preheat oven to 375°F. Thoroughly grease and dust lightly with flour three round 9-inch layer-cake pans.

In a large bowl, cream butter until smooth. Add sugar gradually, beating after each addition. Add lemon extract and stir to blend. Then add egg yolks and beat until light. Sift flour with baking powder and salt. Alternately add flour and milk to the butter-sugar mixture, beating well after each addition. Turn into prepared pans. Bake until cake is golden brown, pulls away from the pan when tipped, and springs back when touched, about 20 to 25 minutes. Remove from oven. Let sit for about 10 minutes. Then turn onto a wire rack to cool. When thoroughly cool, frost with Lemon-Orange Frosting.

$\mathcal{E}$FFIE'S GOLDEN CARROT NUGGETS

makes about 2 dozen 2½-inch cookies

EFFIE THOUGHT THESE COOKIES were much more appropriate for an Easter picnic in gold country than a gold cake would be. While they disappeared off the plate in a flash, Mother's gold cake also turned out to be a favorite gold-country treat, one that lasted all of fifteen minutes once it was cut, with menfolk coming back to see if there was enough left for a second piece.

¾ cup sifted all-purpose flour
⅔ teaspoon baking powder
¼ teaspoon salt
¼ teaspoon freshly grated nutmeg
1 egg
⅓ cup butter or margarine, melted

⅓ cup granulated sugar (don't substitute brown for white)
1 tablespoon grated orange rind
1 tablespoon orange juice, strained
⅓ cup cooked mashed carrots
⅓ cup golden raisins

Preheat oven to 350°F. Grease one large or two small cookie sheets.

Into a medium bowl, sift flour with baking powder, salt, and nutmeg. In a large bowl, beat egg until frothy; add butter and sugar and cream together until light. Stir in orange rind and juice. Blend in carrots. Add flour mixture to egg mixture gradually, then fold in raisins. Drop by teaspoonfuls onto prepared cookie sheets, allowing about 2 inches between cookies. Bake until golden brown and firm to the touch, 10 to 12 minutes. Remove from oven and transfer with a spatula to a wire rack or brown paper to cool.

If cookies are to be eaten within a day or two, store in a covered dish that allows a little circulation of air; for longer storage, seal in double plastic bags and freeze (storage life about 1½ months).

JANE WATSON HOPPING

Spring Thaw: A Tale About Foxes

NOT TOO LONG AGO, when the countryside was pristine and rural folk lived closer to nature, each man, woman, and child held mystic bonds with plant and animal kingdoms, and with the dirt beneath his or her feet. To these folk each winter-barren tree held in its sap the breath of new beginnings—unearthly greens and shadowed branches. And from the earth, shaded gray to black, brown to red, they watched the wonder of grain spring forth, so fragile, and yet the ancient stay against the dark specter of famine.

Early bred to the knowledge of procreation, young and old alike were enthralled by the sight of nature renewing itself: gangling newborn lambs with cotton-wool coats lying in thin sunlight close to their mothers; downy baby chicks, picking at minuscule bits; human babies naked and weak, wrapped up against the cold; curious fawns, nervous baby quail, and wobbly calves in the field, nudging their mother's overflowing bags.

THE COUNTRY MOTHERS COOKBOOK

WHEN I was a little girl, spring was the time of new life and high water on midwestern prairie lands. The mighty Osage River, swelled with runoff from melting snow and rain, flooded out of western Kansas marauding southeast, passed through Missouri, and ended in the Ozark Mountains of Arkansas. Some years it spread five miles from bank to bank, dropping silt over floodplains, leaving them rich and fertile. Such bottom lands were forested and inhabited largely by wild creatures.

In the years when flooding was at its worst, farms washed away and cattle were stranded on high ground or swept downriver. Even more tragic was the plight of the wild critters who before the floods were holed up in dens and in hollow trees all along the riverbanks, and who after the raging waters came were stranded on floating debris.

Our father, who loved all the critters, could hardly wait for the water to subside. He would get out his two large flat-bottomed boats and check them over, making sure they were sound. He and our older brothers would fill them with cages, feed sacks, and tarps, and put in the heavy gloves used for handling trapped animals. At night he would talk to us about God's creatures and our responsibility to them.

Finally Dad would set out with the whole family aboard the well-balanced boats, which were large enough to transport eight people and an equal amount of extra weight. All of us except our two older brothers got into Dad's boat; Ben and Arch rowed the second one.

When our rescue mission got under way, we children were breathless with excitement. As we rowed out into the backwater, we marveled at the dirty waves lapping at the sides of the boat, the ever-moving current flowing as far as the eye could see. Floating in the water were tree tops, big dead logs, boards,

JANE WATSON HOPPING

parts of buildings, pieces of everything you could imagine, and clinging to the debris were critters, young and old alike, stranded too far from shore and too frightened to swim to safety. The most touching sights of all were the newborn creatures, alone, wide-eyed with distress.

One year we found six baby foxes, not much bigger than kittens, holed up in a floating hollow log. They were so starved and frightened that Dad caught them easily and put them in a safe box. Further on we found baby birds in nests, snakes, rabbits, all in bad straits. When the boats were filled up, we rowed in to shore and turned the wild things loose on dry land. We kept the six little foxes, which were much too small to fend for themselves.

At home where we had plenty of tight cages, we made the baby foxes comfortable on some old clothes, and then fed them with a bottle. They adapted like newborn pups. Each one was beautiful beyond imagination: their fur was all shades of brown, gold, orange-tinged with blends of white on peaked ears and bushy tails. They were so gracefully built. In time, as they grew, we had to put them in a stronger walk-in pen about twelve feet square that had a good lock on it.

As spring days passed, we children were busy with farm chores, tending the foxes, and helping our mother incubate off baby chickens. Each year we raised about a hundred pullets to replace the laying hens in the fall and to assure Mother enough pin money to keep up our clothes and buy a few cooking supplies. We raised in a second pen another hundred chickens for meat. By summer we had two large cages full of three-pound chickens. And by this time the foxes were a lovely sight, half grown, about the size of a three-quarter-grown German shepherd and ten times as graceful—sleek as prize animals at a state fair.

Dad, who was skilled at this type of rescue work, knew that the foxes were wild creatures and that there was considerable risk in trying to keep them much longer. Ordinarily, when rescued babies were old enough to fare for themselves, we caged them, loaded them on the wagon and with tears bade them good-bye. Dad and our brothers, Ben and Arch would drive to a likely spot many miles away and turn the animals loose, hoping they would stake out a new territory and not try to return to the farm.

Mother kept cautioning, "It's time." But whenever it came time to take them away, all the family grieved and we children begged, "Not today, not today!" Even so, all of us could see that the foxes were getting restless.

Dad hunted wild rabbits for them daily, but they could smell the chickens nearby and were excited by the scent and fired by instinct to hunt for themselves. Then one night bedlam broke loose. We sat straight up in bed, knowing at once what had happened.

The foxes had overstayed; they had torn a hole in their cage and gotten out. We grabbed lanterns and ran for the chicken pens. The foxes were inside, running wildly about chasing and mauling the chickens, but not eating them. Frantically we tried to stop them or catch them. Dad and the boys did not want to use their rifles, but the chickens were vital to our livelihood for the coming winter. To everyone's relief, Dad and the boys finally caught the foxes and put them into a new tight cage they had been building.

Immediately, without waiting, Mother called a family council; everyone had to attend. The next day we would set the foxes free. All of us sat on our shadowy lantern-lit porch steps—Grandma and Grandpa wrapped in blankets, Mother with her long brown hair in its nighttime braid, Dad looking naked in only his long johns, pants, and boots, and the rest of us in nightclothes that smelled of foxes and chickens—and we sorrowed over the loss of laying hens and meat birds and the near disaster for the foxes.

When we children cried, Dad reminded us that it was only our love for the foxes, which had gotten the upper hand over our good judgment, and had caused this disaster. And Mother put her arms about those of us who were still young and told us that the secret was to learn from such experiences. Grandpa said we weren't the first to learn a lesson the hard way, and talking softly, Grandma reminded us that we would have time to think this all through before spring came, and we would again go out and rescue wild creatures.

JANE WATSON HOPPING

Chicken in the Oven, Chicken in the Pot

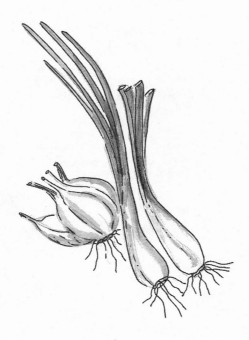

AT THE TURN OF the century, everyone—farmers, doctors, storekeepers, preach-ers—raised chickens for summer meat. By mid to late summer the chickens, raised throughout the spring, were about full grown. Pullets would soon be old enough to lay, and cockerels (young male chickens)—Barred Plymouth Rocks, Buff Orphingtons, Rhode Island Reds, and Langshan—would soon weigh in at eight pounds or more.

In separate pens, Light Brahmas, the largest of all the meat breeds, were nearly as large as a hen turkey. Many breeds excelled Brahmas as egg layers, but for meat production, none could outproduce them. Most cockerels were castrated and sold or used as broilers. Older birds were considered excellent roasters. Standard weights for such huge chickens were cocks, twelve pounds; cockerels, ten pounds; hens, nine and half pounds; pullets, eight pounds.

$\mathcal{E}$ASY-OVER OVEN-FRIED CHICKEN WITH PAN GRAVY

makes 20 pieces of chicken

THIS OLD-FASHIONED WAY TO fix chicken for a potluck or a picnic leaves it nicely browned and not as greasy as a fried bird. When the meat is taken cold to a picnic, or rewarmed at a potluck, the fat and broth are refrigerated for later use, perhaps for making gravy to use in a potpie.

If the chicken is to be served at supper, the broth and drippings are used to make gravy.

2 spring chickens (3-pound store-bought frying chickens will do nicely)
1½ teaspoons salt, slightly more if you wish
Black pepper, as desired

½ cup flour, more if needed
2 eggs, well beaten
2 cups bread crumbs, fresh or dried (preferred)
½ cup butter or margarine, melted
¼ cup boiling stock (see Note)

Preheat oven to 350°F. Thoroughly grease a large baking sheet with 1-inch-deep sides.

Cut the washed chicken into serving-size portions, cutting the breast into 4 pieces. Salt and pepper each piece, dip it in flour, then into beaten eggs, and finally into the bread crumbs. Arrange pieces on the prepared pan; do not overlap. If chicken seems a bit fat, even after all visible fat is removed, cover with foil, loosely so that the chicken does not steam done. (The foil cover also prevents fat and juices from spattering over the oven.) Bake, basting frequently with broth, until chicken is browned nicely and done near the bone, 45 to 50 minutes. Remove from oven and transfer to large platter. Serve hot or cold.

NOTE: To make stock, put the necks, giblets (excluding the liver), and backs into cold, lightly salted water, with a small peeled onion and a bay leaf; simmer until the meat falls off the bone, about 45 minutes. Set off heat to cool.

P AN GRAVY

makes about 2 cups

4 tablespoons all-purpose flour
4 tablespoons pan drippings
1 cup rich milk (skim may be used)

1 cup chicken stock
Sliced mushrooms, optional

In a medium skillet or saucepan, stir flour into melted drippings. Let flour and fat bubble for 3 to 5 minutes, then add milk and stock. Stir constantly until well thickened. If you are adding mushrooms to the gravy, add them now; let simmer in gravy 3 to 5 minutes. Serve gravy over potatoes or rice, or use in a potpie.

A UNT CLARY'S CHICKEN GRUEL

makes about 6 to 8 servings

USUALLY THE WORD "GRUEL" dredges up visions of everything that is unappetizing, fed only to defenseless invalids, old folks, and babies. But here is a gruel that anyone would like.

Bones and trimmings of cold chicken
2 onions, peeled and quartered
1 carrot, peeled and halved
1 bay leaf
2 stalks celery, halved

A sprig of parsley
3 tablespoons cooked rice
1 cup milk or light cream
Salt and pepper, to taste

Put chicken bones and leftover meat in a large saucepan. Cover with cold water and simmer 1 hour. Then add onions, carrot, bay leaf, celery, and parsley. Simmer until the vegetables are soft, then strain them out and put through a fine sieve. Set vegetables aside to cool.

Remove bones and meat from broth; discard bones. Remove all fat possible from broth. Then return vegetables to the broth, add rice, and heat to serving temperature. Just before serving, add milk. Season with salt and pepper to taste.

$\mathcal{A}$UNT CLARY'S BOILED HEN WITH DUTCH DUMPLINGS

makes enough chicken and dumplings for 8 to 10 servings

WHEN WE WERE CHILDREN, Aunt Clary, already old herself and with an even older husband, raised several dozen hens and sold the eggs to those attracted by the sign on her front porch. Besides supplementing their income—mainly gifts from their grown children—with this egg money, she crocheted and sold lace for pillowcases or towels, doilies with a pineapple design, and many other delicate bits of fancy work.

When her hens began to drop off in egg production, at about two years of age, she dressed, cleaned, and boiled them until they were tender, and then added her Dutch dumplings to the pot, turning a loss into a delicious meal.

3- to 4-pound boiling hen (a 4-pound roaster will do nicely if you remove all visible fat)
2 quarts boiling water, more if needed
1 cup skim milk
2 teaspoons salt
½ teaspoon black pepper

1 small onion, peeled and quartered
2 stalks celery, washed and left whole
1 small carrot, peeled and halved lengthwise
1 medium bay leaf
Dutch Dumplings (recipe follows)

In a large kettle or Dutch oven, put chicken, boiling water, and milk (which will whiten the meat). Add salt and pepper, onion, celery, carrot, and bay leaf. Simmer hen slowly for 1½ to 2 hours (simmer a roasting chicken a little less). As the chicken cooks, remove scum which rises to the surface of the broth. (The meat should be submerged as it cooks; weight it down with a plate, if necessary.)

When chicken is tender-done, remove from broth and transfer to a bowl and allow the chicken to cool for 15 minutes at room temperature, then chill. Leave broth in the kettle and set aside to cool until fat rises to the surface; chill; spoon off fat and discard it with vegetables and bay leaf. Refrigerate.

Just before supper, preheat oven to 350°F. Put the bird in a casserole that has a tight cover (you may use foil to cover an open dish), and add ½ *cup* broth. Cover and set in oven to warm while dumplings are being made. At the same time set broth on medium heat to come to a boil. When dumplings are done, remove chicken from oven and set out in the casserole in which it was heated, or transfer to a platter. Spoon dumplings into a deep serving bowl.

JANE WATSON HOPPING

$\mathcal{D}$UTCH DUMPLINGS

3 medium boiling potatoes, peeled,
    cooked, and mashed (about 2
    cups)
1 tablespoon butter or margarine
3 eggs, well beaten

1 teaspoon salt
½ teaspoon black pepper
1 cup all-purpose flour
1 teaspoon baking powder

To the mashed potatoes, add butter and eggs, salt and pepper. Stir in flour and baking powder. Drop by tablespoonfuls into boiling broth. Cover and cook until done when tested with a fork, about 20 minutes. For light dumplings, serve as soon as they are cooked through.

MAGIC LACE AND GOSSAMER

SPUN by fairies in the moonlight,
tangled threads of starshine rare,
woven, as the dawn came creeping,
into cobweb lace and misty gossamer.

—Jane Watson Hopping

THE COUNTRY MOTHERS COOKBOOK

$\mathscr{A}$UNT PEG'S CHICKEN AND RICE PIE

makes about 6 to 8 servings

THIS IS A DELICIOUS way to cook a full-grown hen, as such slow, long cooking tenderizes the meat.

1 large cooked hen (page 76), cut into 10 pieces, with bones removed

2 cups stock (freeze leftover in pint or quart containers for later use)

2 cups cooled cooked long-grain rice

¼ pound mushrooms, cleaned and sliced

1 carrot, peeled and thinly sliced

4 tablespoons butter, plus 1 tablespoon, melted, for rice topping

4 tablespoons all-purpose flour

Juice of 1 lemon

2 teaspoons salt

⅛ teaspoon black pepper

⅛ teaspoon onion powder

3 tablespoons grated Swiss cheese

⅛ teaspoon cayenne pepper

2 eggs, well beaten

Preheat oven to 350°F. Grease thoroughly a 3-quart casserole. Set out chicken, stock, rice, and sliced mushrooms.

To make a gravy, heat *4 tablespoons butter* in a medium skillet until melted, then stir in the flour. Let butter and flour bubble until flour is lightly browned, stirring occasionally. Then add stock, lemon juice, salt, black pepper, and onion powder, stirring continually until gravy has thickened.

To assemble the pie, layer chicken pieces and sliced mushrooms and carrot with hot gravy in a deep 3-quart casserole. In a medium bowl, combine cooked rice with the *1 tablespoon melted butter,* grated Swiss cheese, cayenne pepper, and eggs. Spread rice mixture 2 inches thick over the chicken pie. Bake until nicely browned and heated throughout, about 45 minutes. Serve hot as a main dish.

O the Happy Days of Springtime

IN SPRING, YOU COULD always find Ol' Missus Upjohn wandering through the woods, looking for herbs. Some folks called her an herb doctor, others a midwife. But our grandmother told her children, including our mother, that Alice Upjohn was just a good neighbor with natural healing skills, an old-fashioned woman who loved all of nature—the dew-kissed grasses, flowers, birds, animals, and humans, too. Even neighbors who thought there was something strange about her wanderings said in awe that Alice Upjohn could whistle up any bird song, and talk to wild critters.

WILD MINT TEA

makes 1 cup tea

ALL ALONG THE CREEK banks long-leafed wild mint grows. When stepped on, its fragrance rises up to perfume the air. Old-time women gathered great bouquets of it to dry. In the winter, the dried leaves were used for tea, but in summer the fresh leaves were picked just before use.

About 2 tablespoons (tightly packed) freshly picked wild mint leaves that have been stripped from the stems and washed, gently and quickly, under cold-flowing tap water

1 cup boiling water

To make tea, put prepared leaves in a small kettle and add boiling water. Simmer over medium heat for about 1 minute, then remove from heat and steep for 2 minutes more. Strain into a cup and serve immediately.

CAULIFLOWER AND WATERCRESS SALAD

makes 4 servings

ON THE HUBBARD PLACE there was a large reservoir fed by a free-flowing spring. Early in the season, tender large-leaved watercress grew in abundance, crisp and delicious with just the right bite.

1 medium head cauliflower, washed,
    trimmed, and broken into
    clusters
½ teaspoon salt
1 tablespoon lemon juice, strained,
    plus 1 teaspoon for mayonnaise

1 tablespoon mayonnaise
Lettuce leaves
Watercress sprigs, stems removed

In the morning, boil cauliflower in water to cover with salt and lemon juice. In a small bowl, stir mayonnaise with 1 teaspoon lemon juice until blended. Season with salt and pepper to taste. Chill.

When ready to serve, place a lettuce leaf on each of 4 salad plates and center a cluster of cauliflower on each. Put a teaspoon of lemon mayonnaise into the center. Then stick watercress sprigs into the mounds of cauliflower to look like green and white bouquets.

CHICKEN AND CUCUMBER SALAD WITH LEMON MAYONNAISE

makes 4 to 6 servings

IN THE OLD DAYS women chilled their salad materials in the springhouse, often setting a heavy crockery container in the water and then setting the salad down in the dry crock.

1 quart boned and chopped cooked
   chicken
1 can tiny salad peas

2 cucumbers, peeled and diced
   (remove seeds, if you wish)
Lemon Mayonnaise (recipe follows)

Chill all ingredients before assembling the salad. Then just before serving, combine in a salad bowl and dress with Lemon Mayonnaise.

LEMON MAYONNAISE

makes about ½ cup

½ cup mayonnaise
1 tablespoon lemon juice

Salt and pepper to taste

Blend mayonnaise and lemon juice. Season with salt and pepper to taste. Add desired amount to moisten the salad.

THE TEXT

THE text: Love thou thy fellow man!
　　He may have sinned, One proof indeed,
He is thy fellow, reach thy hand
　　And help him in his need!

Love thou thy fellow man. He may
　　Have wronged thee—then, the less excuse.
Thou hast for wronging him. Obey
　　What he has dared refuse!

Love thou thy fellow man—for, be
　　His life a light or heavy load,
No less he needs the love of thee
　　To help him on his road.

　　　　　　　　　　—James Whitcomb Riley

JANE WATSON HOPPING

Kindness Is Such a Very Simple Thing

OUR MOTHER TAUGHT US at a very early age that we should do unto others as we would have others do unto us. She spoke to us about the old people we saw on the street, alone, without friends or relatives. There but for the Grace of God go I, she told us; and carefully, so we would understand, explained that anyone, even herself, could find him- or herself in such a predicament.

Then she talked to us about her father, our dearly loved Grandpa, and explained that when she was still a child her mother had died, and her father had never deserted any of his children, but raised the small ones alone, and loved them very much. Now that Dad is older, she taught us, it would be wrong to leave him alone, and that is why he lives with us and we share our lives with him.

THE COUNTRY MOTHERS COOKBOOK

$\mathcal{G}$ROUND-BEEF STEW WITH CORNMEAL DUMPLINGS

makes 4 to 6 servings

MOTHER LEARNED TO MAKE this spicy stew from Grandma King, who had run a café in the 1930s. She sold a bowlful of stew with a cup of coffee for ten cents. Sometimes displaced farm folk out of the dust bowl would ask if they could have two spoons and share the stew. Then Grandma would set out a second cup of coffee, fill the bowl to overflowing, and take only a dime for the meal.

STEW

1 pound lean ground meat
½ medium onion, minced
½ bell pepper, minced
2 cloves garlic, peeled and crushed

1 quart canned tomatoes
2 cups water
1 teaspoon oregano
½ teaspoon cumin

TO MAKE STEW

Shape ground beef into 4 large patties; fry in a heavy Dutch oven until rare or medium done; drain off excess fat and break patties in the pan into pieces. Add onion, pepper, and garlic and sauté with meat for a few minutes, until limp. Add tomatoes, water, oregano, and cumin. Simmer, breaking up chunks of tomatoes with the back of a spoon. While the stew cooks, make dumplings.

CORNMEAL DUMPLINGS

½ cup cornmeal
¾ cup all-purpose flour
½ teaspoon salt
1 teaspoon baking powder

2 eggs, lightly beaten
½ cup milk
1 tablespoon butter, melted

TO MAKE DUMPLINGS

In a medium bowl, combine cornmeal, flour, salt, and baking powder; stir to blend. In a smaller bowl, combine eggs, milk, and melted butter. With a spoon, make a well in dry ingredients; pour liquid ingredients into it and stir to blend; don't overstir. Drop batter by teaspoonfuls into the boiling stew, cover pan lightly. Simmer 12 to 15 minutes, or until dumplings are cooked through. Serve immediately, ladling dumplings into soup bowls and covering with stew.

JANE WATSON HOPPING

There Is in Life This Golden Chance

WHEN I WAS A young girl and youthful troubles got the best of me, I would run across the field and let myself through Aunt Mabel's gate, knowing that I would be welcome and that she would give me a glass of milk and a cookie. Then we would walk and walk through her lovely yard and out to the barns, and all about, marveling at the bed of daffodils, looking for wild flowers among the cultivated ones, until finally we would come to the pens where she kept her peacocks and guinea fowl. We would throw them a little grain and call out to them so that they would call back. As they strutted about, we would glory in the colors of their feathers. Then we would wander on to find rocks that looked like eggs or marbles, and some that contained fool's gold. And we talked.

She would tell me tales and family stories, and repeat these lines from "The Golden Chance" by Edgar A. Guest:

> *There is in life this golden chance for every valiant soul,*
> *The unpenned poem or romance, the undiscovered goal.*

With enthusiasm she spoke of the successes that could be mine, if I would just work for them and grow with them. And always when I walked back through Aunt Mabel's gate to go home, I had long forgotten the low spirits that had sent me rushing there in the first place.

Wisdom Gently Spoken

WHEN WE WERE GROWING up, our mother taught us that happiness is a state of mind. She told us: If you can meet life with a cheerful smile and take your knocks as they come without too much complaining, you can be one of the happy people of this world. And you have to develop some kind of "organized common sense."

You have got to work, more than a little bit, and play enough to rest the body and soul. You have to eat good wholesome food with a degree of regularity.

And, she would add, when we were small, our grandma Meekins used to recite to us this little rhyme that she had learned when she was a child:

> *To rise at five, to dine at nine,.*
> *To sup at five, to bed at nine,*
> *Makes a man (or woman) live to ninety and nine.*

The Author in 1947

JANE WATSON HOPPING

86

MOTHER'S STEWED VEAL RUMP WITH VEGETABLES

makes 6 to 8 servings, perhaps with enough leftovers for sandwiches the next day

EFFIE CALLED THIS A delicious pot roast of veal and served it with Baked Potatoes with Dill Butter (page 93).

Broth to cover (see instructions below)

6-pound veal standing rump roast or sirloin with bone

Pork larding fat (may be purchased at butcher shop)

4 large carrots, cut into lengths

3 large onions, cut into fourths, one of them stuck with 3 whole cloves

1 teaspoon salt

½ teaspoon black pepper

1 tablespoon cornstarch

1 tablespoon minced parsley, for garnish

Dusting of paprika

TO MAKE BROTH

Remove bone from meat (or have the butcher do it). In a large kettle put bone (or bones) with 1 teaspoon salt, ½ teaspoon pepper, *1 small* onion, and *1 stalk* celery. Add water to cover amply and simmer until meat remaining on bone is tender, about 1 hour, perhaps a little longer. (Any meat can be picked off bones and used for sandwiches or other recipes.) Drain broth and set aside.

TO PREPARE ROAST FOR STEWING

Lard meat thoroughly by cutting slits into meat and inserting pork fat. In a large Dutch oven, heat at least *3 tablespoons larding fat* (or butter) until very hot, almost smoking; brown roast until it is well sealed and has a good color. Turn off the heat. Add carrots and onions. Cover with broth and add salt and pepper. Cover and simmer gently over slow heat (325°F to 350°F) until the meat is quite tender, 2½ to 3 hours. Turn meat occasionally. Add more liquid if necessary.

When done, transfer meat from pot to a large deep platter. Set pot liquor aside to cool. When fat has risen to the top, remove it, measure broth, and thicken with *1 tablespoon moistened cornstarch* to each cup of broth. Return meat to gravy and heat, adding more salt or pepper if needed. Just before serving, place meat on platter and spoon a little gravy over the top (pour remaining gravy into a gravy boat or a small bowl). Garnish top of meat with minced parsley and dust with paprika.

TINY TENDER, RICH BUTTERMILK BISCUITS WITH HOMEMADE BUTTER

makes about 2½ dozen biscuits

IN LATE SPRING, CREAM from Black Rose (our cow), colored by the cholorophyll in the clovers and grasses she eats, yields up a golden butter that melts in the mouth.

2 cups sifted all-purpose flour
1½ teaspoons baking powder
1 teaspoon salt
½ teaspoon baking soda
⅓ cup butter or margarine

¾ cup buttermilk
¼ cup milk or light cream, for
    brushing the tops of biscuits
Homemade Butter (recipe follows)

Preheat oven to 450°F. Set out a 13 × 11 × 2-inch baking pan.

Into a large bowl, sift flour, baking powder, salt, and soda. With a pastry blender or two knives, cut butter into flour until mixture resembles coarse cornmeal. Make a well in the center of the dry ingredients and add buttermilk all at once. Stir with a fork until dough becomes cohesive, then gently form dough into a ball and place on a lightly floured surface. Knead with fingertips 10 times.

Roll out dough, handling as little as possible, ½ inch thick. Cut out biscuits 1½ to 2 inches in diameter, using a floured cutter or knife. (Even pressure when cutting biscuits keeps their sides straight.) Place biscuits on baking sheet 1 inch apart for crusty sides. Lightly brush tops with milk or cream and bake until light golden brown, about 10 to 15 minutes. Serve with Homemade Butter.

HOMEMADE BUTTER

makes about ½ cup

1 pint heavy cream, warmed to 55°F   1-quart jar with a tight lid
    (cold cream churns slowly)   Salt, to taste

Pour cream into the jar and screw the lid on tightly; wrap in a clean dish towel.
Holding the wrapped jar in both hands, rock it back and forth with a strong,
even motion (concussion separates the butterfat from the milk). First the cream
with look frothy, then thick like whipped cream. In time it will become granu-
lar, then will gather into a cohesive mass. At that point, drain off the buttermilk,
leaving butter in the jar. Fill jar with cold water and shake it to wash milk out
of butter. Pour milky water off; then continue rinsing butter until the water is
clear. Turn butter out into a small bowl and salt to taste. (Leave unsalted for
sweet butter.) Chill and serve with hot biscuits.

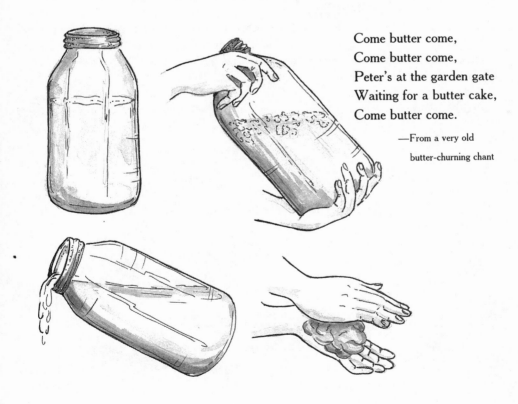

Come butter come,
Come butter come,
Peter's at the garden gate
Waiting for a butter cake,
Come butter come.

—From a very old
butter-churning chant

$\mathcal{M}$ELT-IN-YOUR-MOUTH CHOCOLATE COOKIES

makes about 4 dozen cookies

THIS IS AN EASY "little girl" recipe—easy to make, easy to clean up after. Serve a few while still warm; save the rest to eat later with icy cold milk.

1 cup all-purpose flour
⅓ cup sifted powdered sugar, plus
    ¼ cup for tops of cookies
2 tablespoons cocoa
¼ teaspoon salt

½ cup butter (no substitutes),
    softened at room temperature
1 teaspoon vanilla extract
½ cup lightly salted peanuts

Preheat oven to 300°F. Set out a large cookie sheet.

Into a medium bowl, sift flour, *⅓ cup sugar,* cocoa, and salt. In a second medium bowl, cream butter and vanilla until butter is light. Add flour mixture to butter mixture in fourths, beating smooth after each addition. Fold in peanuts. Drop dough by teaspoonfuls about 2 inches apart onto the cookie sheet. Flatten each cookie to about ⅛-inch thickness with tines of a fork dipped frequently in water; form a crisscross pattern.

Bake until firm to the touch, 12 to 15 minutes. Remove cookies from oven and transfer onto waxed paper, placing cookies close together. Generously sift remaining *¼ cup powdered sugar* over the cookies.

JANE WATSON HOPPING

Ma Loves Me When I'm Good or Bad

From LITTLE GIRLS

GOD made the little boys for fun,
 For rough and tumble times of play;
He made their little legs to run and race
 And scamper through the day.
He made them strong for climbing trees,
 He suited them for horns and drums.
And filled them full of revelries
 So they could be their father's chums.

—Edgar A. Guest

My friend Marie, who has one daughter and six boys of varying ages, often tells me, full of laughter, how ill-prepared she is to deal with a houseful of pure energy unleashed.

$\mathcal{M}$A'S LAYERED MEAT LOAF

makes 8 to 10 servings

WHEN ADA'S SON HENRY was a boy, he swore that his mother's layered meat loaf was the best thing in the world to eat for Sunday dinner. And when he knew that she had made one, he just couldn't keep his mind on the preacher's sermon. Aided and abetted by his stomach, his thoughts wandered around, lost in gastronomical fantasies about Layered Meat Loaf, Baked Potatoes with Dill Butter (page 93), and even about Fancy Buttered Carrots (page 94).

VEAL

1 pound veal, ground
¼ pound fresh pork fat, ground (to moisten very lean veal)
3 soda crackers, crushed
1 tablespoon milk
2 teaspoons lemon juice, strained
1 teaspoon salt
⅛ teaspoon black pepper
1 tablespoon minced onion

PORK

1 pound fresh pork, ground
½ pound smoked ham, ground
2 eggs
½ cup bread crumbs
¼ cup milk
1 teaspoon salt
⅛ teaspoon black pepper

Preheat oven to 350°F. Generously grease a 2-quart loaf pan.

In a large bowl, combine veal, pork fat, crackers, milk, lemon juice, salt, pepper, and minced onion. Using a wooden spoon, blend together or knead together with hands. Pack into the prepared loaf pan.

Combine pork, ham, eggs, bread crumbs, milk, salt, and pepper. Using a wooden spoon, blend together. Pack firmly on top of veal mixture. Bake until well done (170°F when tested with a meat thermometer). Remove from oven and let set for 10 minutes. Remove from the pan, lifting with spatulas, and place on a platter. Serve immediately.

JANE WATSON HOPPING

ℬAKED POTATOES WITH DILL BUTTER

makes 8 to 10 servings

AT OUR HOUSE, WE thought baked potatoes with seasoned butter went with all sorts of main dishes.

8 to 10 medium baking potatoes (select smooth potatoes)
About 3 tablespoons softened butter, for greasing skins of potatoes

Dill Butter (recipe follows)
Salt and black pepper, to taste

Preheat oven to 425°F. Scrub potatoes and remove eyes and any blemishes. Take a little soft butter on your fingers and grease potato skins. Place on an ungreased baking sheet and bake until tender, 45 to 50 minutes. To test for doneness, wrap a kitchen towel around your hand and squeeze the potatoes; if done, they should feel soft. When done, immediately break open the skins to keep them from becoming soggy. Serve promptly, letting each person dress with Dill Butter, salt, and pepper.

𝒟ILL BUTTER

makes enough for 8 to 10 servings

1 stick butter (8 tablespoons), softened at room temperature
¼ teaspoon grated lemon rind

2 teaspoons lemon juice, strained
1 teaspoon minced fresh dill weed (or 1 teaspoon dill seed)

Beat butter until soft; add lemon rind and juice and stir into butter carefully but well. Add minced dill weed. Shape butter into tablespoon-size pats or balls for serving. Chill only until firm.

NOTE: If two tablespoons Dill Butter for each potato seems a more appropriate serving size at your house, double the recipe.

$\mathcal{F}$ANCY BUTTERED CARROTS

makes about 8 servings

ON OLD-TIME FARMS, CARROTS were left in the field to winter over. In spring they were dug and used in pies, breads, puddings, and in simple dishes like this one.

12 medium carrots, peeled but not cut

¼ cup butter, softened at room temperature

1 teaspoon sugar (added to sweeten older carrots)

¼ teaspoon salt

3 tablespoons finely minced fresh parsley

Using fluted cutter, cut prepared carrots crosswise into slices ¼ inch thick. In a large saucepan, bring about 2 inches of water to a boil. Drop carrot slices into the water and cook covered until just tender when pierced with a fork, about 15 minutes. (Check occasionally, adding boiling water as needed so that the carrots do not boil dry.) When done, drain and toss with butter. Season with sugar and salt. Turn carrots into a warm serving dish and garnish with minced parsley. Serve at once.

Long Ago

OUR MOTHER WAS BORN in a log cabin in the hills of southwestern Missouri. She thinks these verses speak faithfully to the love her father bore her mother:

From IKE WALTON'S PRAYER

I crave, dear Lord
  No boundless hoard
  Of gold and gear,
    Nor jewels fine,
    Nor lands, nor kine,
Nor treasure-heaps of anything.—
    Let but a little hut be mine

  Where at the hearthstone I may hear
    The cricket sing,
  And have the shine
  Of one glad woman's eyes to make,
For my poor sake,
    Our simple home a place divine;—
Just the wee cot—the cricket's chirr—
Love, and the smiling face of her.

      —James Whitcomb Riley

SOFT MOLASSES HERMITS

makes about 3½ dozen cookies

THERE IS SOMETHING ABOUT cookies and breads that have been baked in the oven of a wood-burning cook stove that passes all understanding. The flavor and texture have qualities that one can't quite put one's finger on.

1½ cups sifted all-purpose flour	¼ cup butter or margarine
1½ teaspoons baking powder	¼ cup sugar
¼ teaspoon baking soda	1 egg, well beaten
¼ teaspoon salt	½ cup molasses
½ teaspoon ground cinnamon	¼ cup buttermilk
¼ teaspoon ground cloves	½ cup dark raisins

Preheat oven to 400°F. Lightly grease a large baking sheet.

Sift flour a second time with baking powder, soda, salt, cinnamon, and cloves. In a large bowl, cream butter, adding sugar gradually and creaming together until light. Add egg and beat well; then add molasses. Alternately, add flour and milk, stirring only to blend. Fold in raisins. Drop by teaspoonfuls onto the prepared baking sheet, placing about 2 inches apart. Bake until well puffed and firm to the touch, about 10 minutes. Remove from oven and transfer to wire racks or an opened brown paper bag. Cool, then store in an airtight container.

JANE WATSON HOPPING

THE HOME-COMING

THE long, long road lies straight before
Like a dusty ribbon upon the shore
    Till it slippeth down in the valley far,
And leadeth on to the open door
    Where home-lights are.

The light is low in the paling west,
And the bright bird tosses his purple crest,
    No more on wearying wing to roam;
He sees afar his welcome nest;
    He's going home!

There comes a whiff through the deep'ning dark
Of faint wild rose and of balsam bark,
    And so brightly doth the firelight glow,
That, in the dusk, I can almost mark
    The smiles I know!

Oh, bonnie land of joys to be!
Oh, misty heav'n of reverie!
    Dear faces waiting in the gloam,
Pray keep a welcome yet for me;
    I'm coming home!

—Dorothy Cory Stott (Age 16)

(Honor Member)

The Old House

by the Side of the Road

GRANDMA WHITE, WHO WAS so kind and loving to me when I was a young bride, insisted that I bring my washing and come to visit on Wednesdays. If she thought I might forget, she would hang a white dish towel on the fence by the side of the road so I would see it as I passed by and thus be reminded.

A well-organized homemaker, she thought we should begin the washing early. So when I arrived at seven in the morning she would already have the washer loaded with steaming hot water and soap, the starch for our clothes made, and the hand-wash hung on a line in the shade.

After chatting about flowers in bloom, gardens, and making jam, we sorted the clothes. Grandma put the first batch in the washer. As it was finished, she ran the clean clothes through the wringer into a tub of cold rinse water, then back through the wringer into a second tub of cold water, and again through the wringer into a lined wicker basket to be carried out and hung on the clothes-lines.

Grandma, who took great pride in her washing, would insist that I hang the clothes in proper order: colored clothes on the shaded side of the house, so they wouldn't fade; white things in the hot sun to whiten them; good dresses and shirts on hangers under the trees along with the hand-wash.

She thought nothing should be allowed to hang in the sun after it was dry. Therefore, I would run in and out to check the clothes, carefully taking those that were dry off the line, folding them loosely, and putting them in a basket to take into the house.

We would stop at noon for a bit of lunch, then bring in the last of the wash. With cold water, we lightly sprinkled the starched pieces, rolled them tightly, and laid them together in a basket lined with a heavy piece of muslin. We then covered them with a clean bath towel, so the moisture would spread throughout the fabric, thus making it easier to iron out the wrinkles.

We then set up the ironing boards, heating the irons, gathered the hangers, and set them in a spot close to the ironing boards; and we washed and dried the kitchen table so that we would have a clean place on which to stack, as we

JANE WATSON HOPPING

ironed them, pillowcases, dish towels, handkerchiefs, other flat pieces, and folded shirts.

Visiting and ironing throughout the afternoon, we alternately checked the kettle of beans we were cooking for supper. Grandma White did most of the shirts, which she thought had to be ironed wrinkle-free (even the men's work shirts). By midafternoon, we were usually finished (if not, we left the rest to finish up the following day). When there was time, we played cards for a while, just because Grandma loved to, until the men came home, hungry and tired. As Grandpa and Raymond washed up, we set the evening meal on the table. They talked about milk cows, welding, car repairs, and Grandpa's horses; Grandma and I listened and ate, long since talked out, having shared almost everything we could think of.

After supper, I helped clear away and wash the dishes, gathered up the clean, sweet smelling clothes, kissed Grandma, and said good-bye to Grandpa as he went out to the horse barns to feed his registered Morgans. As always, I felt filled by the day, welcomed into my husband's family, warmed by the work and talk, but most of all by the sharing.

THE COUNTRY MOTHERS COOKBOOK

Simple Things and Common Folks

FOR ME, AND A lot of others too, growing up in the early thirties taught us how to love simple things and common folk. Edgar A. Guest speaks to all who care to know about such feelings and experiences:

FOLKS

WE was speakin' of folks, jes' common folks,
　　An' we come to this conclusion,
That wherever they be, on land or sea,
　　They warm to a home allusion;
That under the skin an' under the hide
　　There's a spark that starts a-glowin'
Whenever they look at a scene or book
　　That something of home is showin'.

They may differ in creeds an' politics,
They may argue an' even quarrel,
But their throats grip tight, if they catch a sight
　　Of their favorite elm or laurel.
An' the winding lane that they used to tread
　　With never a care to fret 'em,
Or the pasture gate where they used to wait,
　　Right under the skin will get 'em.

Now folks is folks on their different ways,
　　With their different griefs an' pleasures,
But the home they knew, when their years were few,
　　Is the dearest of all their treasures.
An' the richest man to the poorest waif
　　Right under the skin is brother
When they stand an' sigh, with a tear-dimmed eye,
　　At a thought of the dear old mother.

JANE WATSON HOPPING

It makes no difference where it may be,
  Nor the fortunes that years may alter,
Be they simple or wise, the old home ties
  Make all of 'em often falter.
Time may robe 'em in sackcloth coarse
  Or garb 'em in gorgeous splendor,
But whatever their lot, they keep one spot
  Down deep that is sweet an' tender.

We was speakin' of folks, jes' common folks,
  An' we come to this conclusion,
That one an' all, be they great or small,
  Will warm to a home allusion;
That under the skin an' the beaten hide
  They're kin in a real affection
For the joys they knew, when their years were few,
  An' the home of their recollection.

—Edgar A. Guest

THE COUNTRY MOTHERS COOKBOOK

$\mathcal{A}$UNT MABEL'S BROWN STEW

makes 4 to 6 servings

WHEN I WAS GROWING up, a good brown stew and freshly baked bread was considered a fine supper. Most women, to round out the meal, set out little side plates of sliced peeled turnips or onions, just-picked radishes and green onions, or if no vegetables were available, they opened a jar of home-canned pickles for a little sweet-and-sour.

1½ pounds lean stew meat, diced
1½ teaspoons salt
¼ teaspoon black pepper
¼ cup all-purpose flour
3 tablespoons fat
½ cup chopped onion
1 clove garlic, minced

Boiling water
1 cup peeled and cubed carrots
1½ cups peeled and cubed potatoes
½ cup chopped celery
⅛ teaspoon marjoram
⅛ teaspoon thyme
⅛ teaspoon basil

Cut excess fat off stew meat. Salt and pepper and dredge lightly in flour. Brown in a minimum of fat in a large Dutch oven. (Too much fat makes the stew greasy.) Add chopped onion, a little garlic, and boiling water to cover. Simmer for about 1 hour, or until meat is done but not quite tender. Add carrots, potatoes, celery, and additional water or broth, if needed. Adjust the salt and pepper to taste. Add a sprinkling of herbs—marjoram, thyme, and basil. Simmer until the vegetables are done. The gravy should be fairly thick as the stew finishes and it will burn if not watched. Stir the vegetables about in the gravy, but do not break them up.

OLD-FASHIONED COLLOPS

makes 6 to 8 servings

THE LESTERS, OUR GRANDMOTHER'S people, were early-day pioneers in southern Missouri, and like other settlers had drifted in through the hills of Kentucky, Tennessee, and Virginia. As late as the thirties, we still used Elizabethan words inherited from these descendants of the first English settlers, words like *woods-colt* (a child born out of wedlock), *dauncey,* as in "I feel a might dauncey" (faint); and *collops,* a dish like bacon and eggs, or something cooked over coal, or a piece of anything, especially meat.

2 pounds lean round steak, ground
1 cup cold water
3 tablespoons butter or margarine
3 tablespoons all-purpose flour

1 teaspoon salt
½ teaspoon black pepper
¼ large onion, minced
1 small carrot, diced, optional

In a medium bowl, mix ground meat and water together. Set aside.

In a heavy stew pan, brown butter and flour. Add meat and water mixture, stirring well to prevent lumping. Season with salt and pepper. Add onion (and diced carrot, if you wish). Cover and bring to a boil; cook 5 minutes. Reduce heat and simmer until the meat is tender and the gravy thickened, 35 to 40 minutes. Serve on a platter with a border of boiled rice or mashed potatoes. Garnish with minced parsley.

AUNTIE'S SQUABS WITH GREEN PEAS

makes 3 servings

AUNTIE RAISED GUINEA HENS, peacocks, pigeons, chickens, ducks, geese, and a rare pheasant or two—some for meat, others for pleasure. When I was a young girl, it was a real treat to be invited over for squabs and green peas.

3 squabs
½ pound salt pork, cut into
   ½-inch squares
3 tablespoons butter
2 tablespoons flour
2 cups water, plus 2 quarts for final
   cooking

3 pounds green peas, shelled
2 sprigs parsley
1 green onion
Black pepper to taste
Dusting of paprika, optional

Wash squabs. In a skillet, put cubed salt pork with the butter and fry until light brown. Add squabs to combined fats and brown on all sides until half cooked. Remove squabs and salt pork. Rub flour into the drippings and brown lightly; add *2 cups water* and cook 5 minutes. Then put the contents of the skillet into a Dutch oven with *2 quarts water,* peas, and salt pork. Season with parsley and onion. Cook slowly until peas are partially done, about 10 minutes. Add squabs and black pepper to taste. Continue to simmer until meat is thoroughly cooked, about 20 minutes longer. Remove parsley and onion. Serve squabs and peas on a deep platter, spooning gravy over the top and dusting with paprika.

THE WIND

WHO has seen the wind?
   Neither I nor you.
But when the leaves hang trembling,
   The wind is passing through.

Who has seen the wind?
   Neither you nor I.
But when the trees bow down their heads,
   The wind is passing by.

      —Christina G. Rossetti

JANE WATSON HOPPING

An Old-Time Mother's Day Picnic

WHEN SPRING CAME AND breezes stirred the earth's emerald carpet of grasses, and flowers burst into a profusion of color, Mother always talked to us about Mother's Day get-togethers on the bottomlands along the Osage River. She talked of sparkling streams, blueberries, sumac, and wild nuts blossoming throughout the woodlands, and of the people of her old-time family—grandparents, uncles, aunts, cousins, and friends—and the warm, wonderful times they had together. We, my sister and I, loved to listen to her tales about picnic time in Missouri.

MOTHER would call all of the relatives on our old, black party-line phone: "Come to the old campground for a Mother's Day picnic on Sunday."

We children could hardly wait for the weekend to come. Then on Saturday evening, when the chores were done, Dad would bring out of the carpentry shop his sawhorses, our picnic benches, and half a dozen clean, new 1 × 12-inch boards that he kept stacked and covered. At the picnic site he would set up a large table, using the sawhorses for the base and the boards laid over them for a tabletop.

Grandpa, usually with Freddie tagging along, would come out of the barn with his long hay rope rolled up over his arm, carrying the horseshoes and pegs. At camp he would make swings in the trees for all the children. Then with a warning to leave it alone, he laid out his rifle, rolled in a worn-out quilt, and shells, which would be used for protection from viperous snakes or rabid varmints, and for hunting. Our brother Ben, who always claimed the baseball and bat Dad had made for all of us, would run out with them and lay them on his personal pile of gear.

We girls were the first to bring out our cane fishing poles. We all had cans for worms and even the youngest dug their own bait. Grandma, sitting in her rocker on the porch, watched, telling each of us as we ran by, "catfish, crappies, and brook trout will be big enough to eat by now, and there will be plenty of

JANE WATSON HOPPING

game," She always got excited thinking about having fresh fish, rabbits, squirrels, and a big snapping turtle for the picnic and some extra wild meat for the week to come.

Mother gathered up the usual picnic gear, including our big over-the-campfire coffeepot and the coffee to put in it. She spent all evening baking and cooking. Then about bedtime she would remind all of us children that at this time of year, the creek would be nice and clear from the last rain, and that if we wanted to play in it, we would have to take an old dress or pair of overalls. Dad, who came into the house when it got dark, promised us a fair warm day.

The next morning, all of the children in our many families got up early to do chores. At our house, we girls raced downstairs before our mother could get out of bed and fixed breakfast for her and for all the rest of the family. After breakfast, I went out to throw wheat to the chickens, while Ben gave the hogs a bushel of corn.

Dad and Grandpa turned out the extra horses. Princess and Pet, the two best horses we had for pulling the wagon, stepped around a bit when the boys fed and watered them at the barn. They had taken us picnicking so many times that they seemed to know where they were going and were eager to get started. (On picnic day they got an extra ration of grain.)

About seven o'clock, we started packing everything in the wagon; by nine we were all sitting on fresh hay in the bed of the wagon or on the box, ready to go. It took about one hour, bumping along over a country road, to get to the old campground where we picnicked.

As was our custom, whoever arrived first started making camp: gathering wood, making a rock stove so there would be fresh coffee for folks who had come a long distance—some had started about daylight. Soon the wagons would begin to pull into the campground, family by family, and sometimes there would be thirty-five or more men, women, and children. Grandfathers and big boys would hop out to unload the wagons, and fathers immediately set up family campfires and tables.

Women moved from camp to camp, hugging loved ones not seen near often enough. Children of all ages, whooping like wild things, ran in packs, hither and yon, and wrestled with cousins on the grass. The campground, as it filled, became an area of gentle bedlam, happy shouted greetings, firm callused handshakes, kisses freely given (even for half-grown boys who ran away, pleased but embarrassed). And there was nonstop talking. Men moved restlessly about, stopping to talk to brothers, fathers, or uncles who lived far enough away so that they had not visited in person for a while; and they shared coffee from camp to camp, and ate huge pieces of cake or handfuls of cookies, given them along with little hugs and a peck on the cheek from the womenfolk.

THE COUNTRY MOTHERS COOKBOOK

Then, almost as though they had forgotten their duties, mothers began to hand out cups of milk and cookies to children who were getting hungry, and check babies still held by other children in the family. Many sat down right then and with a shawl thrown over one shoulder, let the infants nurse. As the babies were diapered and fed, they would be put to bed in large clothes baskets, which were padded with cuddly comforters, then covered all over with mosquito netting to keep off bugs.

Women with older children took them all out into a nice sunny spot so that they could all get reacquainted and could meet friends their cousins had brought along with them to share in the picnic. As the children began to run and play together, some of the women would go back to their family campsites, leaving only a couple of mothers to visit and keep an eye on the children.

GIVE ME THE BABY

GIVE me the baby to hold, my dear—
    To hold and hug, and to love and kiss.
Ah! he will come to me, never a fear—
    Come to the nest of a breast like this,
As warm for him as his face with cheer.
Give me the baby to hold, my dear!

Trustfully yield him to my caress.
    "Bother," you say! What! "a bother" to *me?*—
To fill up my soul with such happiness
    As the love of a baby that laughs to be
Snuggled away where my heart can hear!
Give me the baby to hold, my dear!

Ah, but his hands are grimed, you say,
    And would soil my laces and clutch my hair.—
Well, what would pleasure me more, I pray,
    Than the touch and tug of the wee hands there?—
The wee hands there, and the warm face here—
Give me the baby to hold, my dear!

—James Whitcomb Riley

JANE WATSON HOPPING

In time, horseshoe pegs were in place and an easygoing old men's contest would be started. The swings were hung in the trees, little girls began to argue with boys over who would have the first turn; it was the same at the teeter-totters the men had put up. Some boys went fishing, others went down to the swimming hole. Pass the word, they would say, we're going skinny-dipping! Everywhere, children and grownups alike played hopscotch and hide-and-seek among the trees, running and laughing together. In grassy spots, little girl cousins played farmer-in-the-dell for hours, going round and round and round, then resting on the grass.

And, here and there, folks played old-time music and sang songs: "He traced her little footprints in the snow . . ." and "Life is like a mountain railroad with an engineer that's brave, you must make the run successful from the cradle to the grave . . . ," or even verse after verse of the old American ballad "Red River Valley," of which Carl Sandburg has said, "I have heard it sung as if bells might be calling across a mist in the gloaming." My grandmother's personal favorite was "Two Little Girls in Blue."

Sooner or later, someone would strike up a little square dancing music. Young marrieds would twirl and spin and stamp their feet amid gales of laughter, and courting couples would dance with them, or wander off into fields of wild flowers, oblivious to the music.

By midday or a little after, all the hard play began to take its toll. Parents called over the sound of excited winners of games, "Don't hide too far away. Don't swing too high!" Little ones fussed and older children begged for food. The women comforted their smaller children and handed the older ones a snack. Fishermen—men, women, boys, and girls—straggled back into camp to show off their catch. Other men and boys brought in game, some for cooking, some to be washed and chilled in the icy creek water, salted, and then packed in a canning kettle or roast pan and set down in the cold water to chill until they started home.

Our older sister Mabel always made her Dutch-oven fricasseed chicken and cooked it in the ashes and coals of the campfire; other women at family campfires fried fish, rabbit, and squirrel. Our auntie baked buttermilk biscuits in a big Dutch oven. She raked ash and coals up around the filled pot and put more ash and coals on the lid.

When the time was right, Grandma would call out "Paw, it's time to fix the taters." He would wrap a whole bushel basket of red spuds in clay and lay them in the ashes of the fire to bake.

When the fragrance of woodsmoke, cooking meat, and coffee wafted all through the camp and woods, and as the food began to finish cooking, men and boys went to the creek to wash their faces and hands. They saw to it that the children did the same, then took their places at the tables, usually with a small child on one knee and another sitting close by on the bench. The women and girls set out the food, then one by one sat at the table. Grace was said all through the camp, but no one criticized those families that couldn't wait and just started passing the food around.

After the feast, by about three o'clock, some folks had their wagons packed, mostly the families with small children, old folks, and a long drive home. Leave-taking began with lingering handclasps and kisses; middle-aged folks got teary when tenderly hugging the old folks; children started up games with no ending and kept playing even when parents called. Eventually our family with just one or two others would be left.

Grandpa would take the swings down and roll up his rope; Dad and the older boys loaded the wagon. Mother laid quilts over the straw so we younger ones could lie down on it. Dad, as usual, made his mother comfortable so the wagon's jolting would not make her bones ache. Before long we would all be dreaming, lulled by the wagon's gentle, steady movement. But even those of us who were dozing on the long ride home knew when we were close to home —we could feel Princess and Pet step up their pace. We would all clamber out of the wagon, tired but happy, wondering what delights next year's Mother's Day picnic would bring.

JANE WATSON HOPPING

OUT FISHIN'

A feller isn't thinkin' mean,
  Out fishin';
His thoughts are mostly good an' clean,
  Out fishin'.
He doesn't knock his fellow men,
Or harbor any grudges then;
A feller's at his finest when
  Out fishin'.

The rich are comrades to the poor,
  Out fishin';
All brothers of a common lure,
  Out fishin'.
The urchin with the pin an' string
Can chum with millionaire an' king;
Vain pride is a forgotten thing,
  Out fishin'.

A feller gits a chance to dream,
  Out fishin';
He learns the beauties of a stream,
  Out fishin';
An' he can wash his soul in air
That isn't foul with selfish care,
An' relish plain and simple fare,
  Out fishin'.

A feller has no time fer hate,
  Out fishin';
He isn't eager to be great,
  Out fishin'.
He isn't thinkin' thoughts of pelf,
Or goods stacked high upon a shelf,
But he is always just himself,
  Out fishin'.

A feller's glad to be a friend,
  Out fishin';
A helpin' hand he'll always lend,
  Out fishin'.
The brotherhood of rod an' line
An' sky and stream is always fine;
Men come real close to God's design,
  Out fishin'.

A feller isn't plotting schemes,
  Out fishin';
He's only busy with his dreams,
  Out fishin'.
His livery is a coat of tan,
His creed—to do the best he can;
A feller's always mostly man,
  Out fishin'.

—Edgar A. Guest

THE COUNTRY MOTHERS COOKBOOK

An Embarrassment of Carp

ON MOTHER'S DAY OUR family, avid fishermen and fisherwomen all, used to go down to the sloughs for a picnic and some serious fishing. My father, grandfather, an uncle or two, and several aunts spread out along the bank at various holes to fish all day. We cousins played from early morning until dark, alternately under the supervision of an aunt or mother—the rest were all casting bait.

One day Grandpa, who had a passion for fishing and who was frugal to a fault, came running back down the bank, slipping in the mud, so excited his face flamed as bright as his graying red hair. He had come on a hole of spawning carp—a trash fish filled with bones. But since they were huge and in good shape, he had gotten down into the water and somehow killed enough of them to fill a gunnysack. Mother didn't say anything; she just accepted his catch in the high spirit it was given.

When we got home, Mother and Grandma had to "figure out" what to do with the carp. Finally they decided to pressure-can them to soften the bones so we could eat them. All that winter Mother prepared them every way she could think of, including putting a cream sauce over them. Wisely, she served hot, feather-light biscuits with creamed carp for those of us who were not overly fond of it.

From BROAD RIPPLE

THE river's story flowing by,
Forever sweet to ear and eye,
Forever tenderly begun—
Forever new and never done.
Thus lulled and sheltered in a shade
Where never feverish cares invade,
I bait my hook and cast my line,
And feel the best of life is mine.

—James Whitcomb Riley

JANE WATSON HOPPING

THE COUNTRY MOTHERS COOKBOOK

CREAMED CARP
AND CARP À LA CHAMBORD

makes about 4 servings

GRANDPA LOVED ANYTHING WITH gravy (which is what country folk call any sauce). And, no matter how often Mother fixed Creamed Carp for supper, he ate it with gusto.

2 tablespoons butter or margarine
2 tablespoons all-purpose flour
½ cup fish stock (see note) or
    1 crushed chicken bouillon cube
    in ½ cup boiling water

½ cup heavy cream
½ teaspoon salt
⅛ teaspoon ground black pepper
1 pound cooked carp (a 1-pound
    can of light pink salmon will do)

Preheat oven to 350°F. Set out a medium heatproof dish with cover.

In a small skillet, melt butter; add flour and stir until blended, about 3 minutes. Then slowly add stock and cream, stirring constantly. When thickened, add salt and pepper. Meanwhile, in the oven or under the broiler, warm fish in a heatproof covered dish. Pour the sauce over the warmed fish and garnish with fresh parsley.

NOTE: In a covered saucepan, simmer fish bones for about 8 minutes; drain and reserve ½ cup stock.

CARP À LA CHAMBORD

IN LATER YEARS MOTHER found this recipe, and we have laughed many a time about Grandpa's carp, that we thought of as edible by necessity, never knowing that to some it was a delicacy.

REMOVE LIVER AND CHOP it with parsley and mix with bread crumbs, 2 or 3 shallots, salt, and pepper. Stuff the carp with this mixture. Then place in a fish kettle with three tumblers of dry white wine, two tumblers of water or more if needed to cover the fish. Allow to simmer gently for an hour and a half, then remove the fish from the sauce and lay on a platter. Add to the sauce 6 ounces of butter, 2 tablespoons espagnole sauce. Reduce same, then pour over fish and serve. Truffles or mushrooms may be added to the sauce.

JANE WATSON HOPPING

DEVILED SALMON WITH MEDIUM WHITE SAUCE AND MASHED-POTATO MERINGUE

makes about 6 servings

ON A YELLOWED NEWSPAPER clipping dated 1913, which was tucked into our great-grandma's For-Man-and-Beast-Doctor book, we found this recipe. And once the women began to make it for late suppers, it became a favorite quick-to-make dish that showed up on dinner tables (at noon) and even at breakfast tables early in the morning.

Medium White Sauce (recipe
    follows)
Mashed-Potato Meringue (recipe
    follows)
1 can salmon (pink or red will do
    nicely)
2 hard-cooked eggs, shelled

1 tablespoon minced parsley
½ teaspoon salt
¼ teaspoon black pepper
1 tablespoon lemon juice, strained
Butter, as desired
    (2 or 3 tablespoonfuls)

In order to assemble this dish quickly, make white sauce and mashed-potato meringue before preparing salmon mixture. Cover warm ingredients and set aside until needed. Preheat oven to 350°F. Grease a medium baking dish.

Mince salmon (remove bones and skin if you wish; however, when left in, they add minerals to the diet). Add yolks of eggs, mashed fine, and parsley. Season with salt and pepper and stir in the lemon juice. Turn into prepared baking dish. Chop egg whites and add to prepared white sauce; pour sauce over salmon and cover with a thick meringue of mashed potatoes. Dot with butter and bake until potatoes are lightly browned, 35 to 40 minutes. Serve with a salad for dinner or supper.

THE COUNTRY MOTHERS COOKBOOK

MEDIUM WHITE SAUCE

makes about 2 cups

2 tablespoons butter, melted
2 tablespoons all-purpose flour
2 cups milk, skim will do nicely

¼ teaspoon salt, more as desired
⅛ teaspoon black pepper

In a heavy saucepan, combine melted butter with flour; add milk and stir continually until thick. Salt and pepper to taste (don't add to much of either).

MASHED-POTATO MERINGUE

makes about 2 cups meringue

2 cups hot mashed cooked potatoes
½ cup milk or light cream, more as
   needed

1 teaspoon salt
¼ teaspoon black pepper

Into mashed potatoes, whip milk and season with salt and pepper.

$\mathcal{E}$FFIE'S BROILED FISH WITH PARSLEY AND LEMON BUTTER

makes 4 servings

WHEN EFFIE, THE FIRST woman in the family to have an oven with a broiler in it, began to broil fish, all of the women copied her recipes and tucked them safely away until they too had a new stove.

4 salmon steaks, about ¾ inch thick
2 tablespoons butter, melted
Salt and black pepper as desired

Parsley and Lemon Butter (recipe follows)

Turn heat in broiler to 550°F for at least 10 minutes before beginning to broil fish. Brush steaks with butter and sprinkle with salt and pepper. Lay steaks on a greased broiler pan. Turn broiler down to 450°F. Place the pan in broiler so that fish is about 2 inches from the heat. Turn steaks over at least once, cooking 3 to 5 minutes on each side, depending on size and thickness of steaks. Serve with Parsley and Lemon Butter.

$\mathcal{P}$ARSLEY AND LEMON BUTTER

1 stick (¼ pound) butter or
    margarine, softened at room
    temperature
2 tablespoons minced parsley

Juice and finely grated rind of half
    or whole lemon
½ teaspoon salt
¼ teaspoon black pepper

To the butter, add parsley, grated rind and lemon juice, salt, and pepper. Combine well and set aside until needed. The seasoned butter should be used at room temperature so that it readily melts over the fish.

OLD-FASHIONED SOUSED FISH

1 whole fish or fish fillets
White or cider vinegar
2 onions, sliced
½ teaspoon salt

¼ teaspoon whole allspice
¼ teaspoon cloves
¼ teaspoon minced ginger

Lay fish in an ovenproof glass baking dish. Pour vinegar over to cover. Add sliced onions, salt, and spices. Bake covered in a 350°F oven for 1 hour. Remove the dish from the oven and let fish cool in the liquid. Chill. Serve on a lettuce leaf, garnished with parsley.

OUR MOTHER

HUNDREDS of stars in the pretty sky,
   Hundreds of shells on the shore together,
Hundreds of birds that go singing by
   Hundreds of bees in the sunny weather;

Hundreds of dew drops to greet the dawn,
   Hundreds of lambs in the purple clover
Hundreds of butterflies on the lawn,—
   But only one mother the wide world over.

—Anonymous

JANE WATSON HOPPING

Mother's Day

OUR MOTHER TAUGHT US many things by example, then sometimes she simply laid her wisdom before us and let us feast upon it if we would. She loved poetry and wrote a bit of verse herself, sharing her favorite songs with us, the gems of life, like the poem "Tale of a Brooch" (page 120).

TALE OF A BROOCH

A little woman found a brooch
  upon the street one day;
It looked to her like jewelry the
  10-cent stores display.
She took it home to pin her waist
  while out to wash she went,
And day by day that trinket gleamed
  as o'er the tub she bent;
But no one stopped to notice it. No mistress at the door
Would cast a second glance at things the washerwoman wore.

"It is a pretty brooch," she thought. "I'll wear it while I may,
Then give it to my daughter on her graduation day.
It's rather sad to look at now; I've lost a pearl or two,
But I can pay a jeweler to make it good as new."
So when the happy time arrived she asked a man the cost
Of two small pearls which would replace the ones that she had lost.

The jeweler the trinket took and gravely looked it o'er.
Said he: "Wait just a moment, please; I fear 'twill cost you more
Than you expect. These pearls are rare." She trembled at his speech.
"For gems like this we'll have to charge two thousand dollars each.
This is a most expensive brooch, exquisite, charming, quaint!"
The washerwoman heard no more. She'd fallen in a faint.

To find that brooch police had searched the city up and down,
And all the time it glistened on a woman's gingham gown,
And all the time it glistened as she toiled some floor to scrub
Or shed its rays of loveliness above the steaming tub.
But like this washerwoman, countless folks, year in, year out,
Perhaps are blessed with riches they have never learned about.

—Edgar A. Guest

JANE WATSON HOPPING

120

Little Girl, O So Sweet

ONE FINE SPRING DAY, when playgrounds were again alive with children, I saw two lovely little girls about three or four years old at play in a park. Looking at their golden hair and baby ways, I wondered where their mother could be. Then an older boy who looked to be about eight or ten ran over to them, took their hands, and led them to an area where young mothers watched small children at play. He settled down close by, getting up now and again to swing them or to wipe dirt off their hands and clothing.

That scene reminded me of my husband's memories of sitting at his grandmother's knee, being taught the important responsibility of the oldest child in the family to the youngest, of the duty of the strong to the weak. It is a lesson he never forgot.

THE COUNTRY MOTHERS COOKBOOK

ANN'S EASY-TO-MAKE STAR COOKIES

makes about 3 dozen thin cookies

THIS OLD-TIME RECIPE MAKES enough to keep lots of hungry little ones happy for an afternoon.

½ cup butter or margarine,
    softened at room temperature
1 cup sugar, plus ½ cup for
    sprinkling on cookies
1 egg, beaten to a froth

2 tablespoons heavy cream
½ teaspoon vanilla extract
1¾ cups sifted all-purpose flour
2 teaspoons baking powder
½ teaspoon salt

Preheat oven to 375°F. Set out a large baking sheet.

In a large bowl, cream butter and *1 cup sugar* until light. Add egg, cream, and vanilla; stir until well blended. Sift flour with baking powder and salt; gradually stir into butter mixture. Cover bowl and chill dough for at least 30 minutes.

Turn dough out onto a lightly floured, smooth surface. Roll out ⅛ inch thick (for a little cook, roll out ¼ inch thick). Using a star cutter, cut out cookies. Sprinkle as needed with *½ cup sugar*. Place cookies on the baking sheet and bake until light brown around the edges, about 8 minutes.

COUNTING THE STARS

I tried so hard to count the stars,
    And got as far as three,
When many others slyly peeped,
    And, smiling, blinked at me.

So I began it o'er again,
    And got as far as nine,
When all at once I seemed to see
    A thousand others shine.

Then came so many in the sky,
    I would not try again;
For all the counting that I know
    Is only up to ten.

—Mary Brownson Church

JANE WATSON HOPPING

YOUNG ELIZABETH'S FRUIT AND NUT CHOCOLATE ICEBOX COOKIES

makes about 12 dozen cookies

IN THE THIRTIES AND even later, some homes still had iceboxes instead of refrigerators. Old-time women often kept icebox cookie dough on hand, ready to slice and bake when company came or when the family begged for a little sweet.

4 cups sifted, all-purpose flour, plus
    1 tablespoon for lightly dusting
    fruit and nuts
3½ teaspoons baking powder
1½ teaspoons salt
1 cup butter or margarine, softened
    at room temperature
1½ cups sugar

2 eggs, unbeaten
4 squares unsweetened chocolate,
    melted
1 teaspoon vanilla extract
½ cup broken walnuts
½ cup pitted dates, cut with scissors
½ cup raisins, cut with scissors

Into a medium bowl, sift *4 cups flour* with baking powder and salt. In a large bowl, with a spoon, beat butter, sugar, eggs, chocolate, and vanilla until thoroughly blended. In a small bowl, combine nuts, dates, and raisins. Stir in *1 tablespoon flour;* using the fingers as a sieve, shake off excess flour, until fruit and nuts are very lightly coated. Fold fruit and nuts into the butter-sugar mixture. Add *4 cups flour* gradually, mixing well after each addition.

Divide dough into two portions; shape into rolls, 2 inches in diameter. Roll each portion in waxed paper or foil (or pack into cookie molds). Refrigerate until firm.

Preheat oven to 350°F. Before slicing, let rolls stand at room temperature for 25 minutes, or until dough is soft enough to dent when pressed with a fingertip. Using a sharp knife, cut rolls into thin slices ⅛ to ¼ inch thick. Bake until crisp and firm to the touch, about 10 minutes. Cool baked cookies on kraft paper (an opened brown bag will do). When thoroughly cool, store those for immediate use in an airtight container. Store the balance in double-wrapped freezer bags (will keep frozen for about 2 months); or store raw dough wrapped in foil overnight in refrigerator or for about 2 months in the freezer for later use.

$\mathcal{N}$ELLY'S FIRST CUPCAKES

makes 12 cupcakes

THIS IS A LITTLE girl's recipe. She may need help, particularly when separating eggs or baking.

1 cup sifted all-purpose flour	1 tablespoon grated orange rind
¼ teaspoon salt	½ cup sugar
1 teaspoon baking powder	4 egg yolks, well beaten
4 tablespoons butter or margarine	¼ cup milk

Preheat oven to 350°F. Thoroughly grease a 12-cup muffin pan with medium cups.

   Into a medium bowl, sift flour with salt and baking powder three times. In a large bowl, cream butter until light; add orange rind. Gradually add sugar to butter and rind, creaming mixture together until fluffy. Then add egg yolks and blend well. To butter-sugar mixture, add flour alternately with milk, beating after each addition. Spoon batter into prepared cups, filling ⅔ full. Bake until well risen, golden brown, and firm to the touch, about 18 minutes.

From MARJORIE'S ALMANAC

ROBINS in the tree top,
   Blossoms in the grass,
Green things a-growing
   Everywhere you pass;
Sudden little breezes,
   Showers of silver dew,
Black bough and bent twig
   Budding out anew;
Pine tree and willow tree,
   Fringed elm, and larch,—
Don't you think that May-time's
   Pleasanter than March?

—Thomas Bailey Aldrich

JANE WATSON HOPPING

Knee-deep in June

JUNE, THAT MONTH FAVORED of all the year, when spring ends and summer bursts upon the landscape, when trees and shrubs delight the eye and flowers display the richness of their dress, when the fragrance of roses perfumes the air and fruit swells on the bough. June is so lovely that poets of every ilk and age have sung her praises, and none with so much joy as James Whitcomb Riley in the following verses titled "A Water-Color":

Low hidden in among the forest trees
    An artist's tilted easel, ankle-deep
In tousled ferns and mosses, and in these
    A fluffy water-spaniel, half asleep
        Beside a sketch-book and a fallen hat—
        A little wicker flask tossed into that.

A sense of utter carelessness and grace
    Of pure abandon in the slumb'rous scene,—
As if the June, all hoydenish of face,
    Had romped herself to sleep there on the green,
        And brink and sagging bridge and sliding stream
        Were just romantic parcels of her dream.

           —James Whitcomb Riley

SEVEN TIMES ONE

THERE'S no dew left on the daisies and clover,
    There's no rain left in heaven;
I've said my "seven times" over and over,
    Seven times one are seven.

I am old, so old I can write a letter;
    My birthday lessons are done;
The lambs play always, they know no better;
    They are only one times one.

O moon! in the night I have seen you sailing,
    And shining so round and low;
You were bright! ah, bright! but your light is failing, —
    You are nothing now but a bow.

You moon, have you done something wrong in heaven
    That God has hidden your face?
I hope, if you have, you will soon be forgiven,
    And shine again in your place.

O velvet bee, you're a dusty fellow,
    You've powdered your legs with gold!
O brave marshmary buds, rich and yellow,
    Give me your money to hold!

And show me your nest with the young ones in it, —
    I will not steal it away;
I am old! you may trust me, linnet, linnet, —
    I am seven times one today!

               —Jean Ingelow

Her Smile of Cheer and Voice of Love

WHEN AUNT CLARY WAS young, she was a playful mother. She could easily be coaxed by her children to leave her chores and come outside to play. And when they all played hide-and-seek, run-sheep-run, kick-the-can, and other boisterous, laughter-filled games, she ran like the wind, her long skirt whipping about her legs, the pins falling out of her long chestnut hair—after which all the children would help her search about the playyard for the pins she needed to put her hair back up again.

When she played with the little ones, she sang in her lovely rich voice "The Farmer in the Dell" and took her turn in the center of the ring of children, and she sang and played "London Bridge" with vigor, falling at the appropriate time to the grass with a thump, much to the delight of her youngsters.

She was a "holding" mother, who loved to have her babies on her lap. She sang lullabies and would play patty-pan with them, and peek-a-boo, singing, "peek-a-boo, peek-a-boo, I see you hiding there! Peek-a-boo, peek-a-boo, hiding behind the chair," to make them laugh.

Sometimes her mother, aunts, sisters, or sisters-in-law would scold her a mite about her house that was forever strewn with toys: dolls asleep in chairs, battered railway cars that, as soon as a young conductor returned, would run on imaginary tracks across the painted floors, and tables littered with paint

THE COUNTRY MOTHERS COOKBOOK

boxes. About the house lay books marked by young readers, who would in time sit down to read again.

The sweetest-smelling room in her house was the kitchen, where she and her girls, even the little ones, baked cookies, breads, cakes and roasted meat and other good things. On top of the stove, fragrant pots of soup or beans simmered. Piles of dishes were washed sparkling clean by industrious young hands, as each girl took her turn at cleanup. A toy ironing board and small tubs waited for wash days that came as regular as clockwork.

Despite the endless daily chores, the quick imaginative games and the romping, bright-eyed play in the farmyard and out into the fields, the evenings were quiet, filled with gentle silences and echoes of a joy-filled day. About the house, toys were tucked in boxes, doll-babies slept in homemade cradles beside the beds of their little mothers, or safely in their arms, paint boxes and books were stacked neatly on the table, ready for another day's use.

Then in the soft light of a coal oil lamp, Aunt Clary, an avid reader, would bask in the quiet, or read to her husband and older children long passages from famous American writers of the day, newspaper copy about a president newly elected to office, about street lamps and homes that now had Edison's new light, Ford motorcars made on an assembly line, and new machinery that would revolutionize agriculture.

And she read passages from the Bible, encouraged conversation about the love of God, creativity, caring and sharing, honesty, truth, honor, and ambition. She listened thoughtfully while her young sons and her husband aggressively shared their points of view.

Sometimes she would recite a newly learned bit of poetry such as the following:

HEROISM

HE, who, framing the nation's laws,
Thinks not of self, but of her cause
   Should be deemed a hero.

He who fights for his country's cause,—
Freedom and right and guarded laws,—
   Should be deemed a hero.

He, who, leading a righteous life,
Doth guard the land from crime and strife,
   Should be deemed a hero.

Aye, he who, to his duty true,
Doeth the best that he *can* do,
   Should be deemed a hero.

—Eleanor M. Sickles (Age 13)

(Silver Badge Winner)

JANE WATSON HOPPING

128

ℒITTLE DARLIN' COOKIES

makes about 5 dozen cookies

DELICIOUS TO A FAULT, these crisp cookies, which break easily, are made from a pattern recipe, one that was commonly learned by little girls between ages six and ten. It can be made plain or with very finely chopped nuts sprinkled over the top of each cookie. Sometimes we stir in the nuts, which gives a nice crunch to the cookies.

2 sticks (½ pound) sweet butter (no
    substitutes), softened at room
    temperature
1 cup sugar

2 cups all-purpose flour
½ cup finely chopped nuts, almonds
    or walnuts preferred (optional)

Preheat oven to 350°F. Lightly grease a cookie sheet.

In a large bowl, cream butter until light. Beat in sugar gradually. Then add flour and mix well. Add nuts if desired. Turn dough onto a lightly floured, flat surface; roll or pat into ½-inch thickness. Cut dough into 1-inch round cookies. Place 1½ inches apart on the prepared cookie sheet. Bake until pale golden, 10 to 15 minutes. Remove from oven; let cookies cool about 1 minute on cookie sheet. Then transfer carefully to a wire rack or brown paper. When cool, store in an airtight container.

Strawberries, Soft Cheeks Turned to the Sun

GREAT-GRANDPA PEAK LOVED TO grow strawberries. Mother recalls when she was about five helping him pick large, plump berries while he told her about the wild strawberries in the woods of his youth. The sweet, juicy berries they were picking out of his patch had been domesticated for only about a hundred years or so, and as they worked, searching among the heavy leaves for the ripest fruit, he taught her how to grow abundant crops.

His favorite varieties were Ozark Beauty and Ogallalas, both of which were ever-bearing—that is, producing generous amounts of berries per acre on vigorous vines from late May well into the fall. "Look, sissy," he would say as he showed her the differences between the two types. Ozark Beauties are unusually large and firm, and Ogallalas have a keen wild strawberry flavor. Both types were and are favorites on our family's table.

JANE WATSON HOPPING

$\mathscr{A}$DA'S OLD-TIME STRAWBERRY SHORTCAKE

makes 4 large or 6 medium-size servings

IN STRAWBERRY COUNTRY YOU can smell ripe berries from the onset of warm days in late May until mid-June. Our friend Bill grew them so big, sweet, and juicy that a woman could hold only three in the palm of her hand. In late June, when the picking was almost finished and the berries were ripening fast in the warm summer sun, he would stop by the house with several crates—some for jam, some for freezing, and a generous amount for strawberry shortcakes.

handwritten: > use as Biscuit — cut into wedges for breakfast

1 quart fresh strawberries, hulled
1 cup sugar, plus 2 tablespoons for
    the shortcake
2 cups sifted all-purpose flour
1 tablespoon baking powder
1 teaspoon salt
⅓ cup cold butter or margarine,
    plus ¼ cup softened at room
    temperature for buttering
    shortcake

1 cup milk
Light cream or Sweetened Whipped
    Cream (page 17)

handwritten: → I used ¾ cup skim ¼ cup Buttermilk

Slice strawberries, sprinkle with *1 cup sugar,* and let stand 1 hour.

Preheat oven to 450°F. Grease an 8-inch round layer-cake pan; set it aside until needed. Into a medium bowl, sift flour with remaining *2 tablespoons sugar,* baking powder, and salt. Using a pastry blender or two dinner knives, cut in *⅓ cup cold butter* until mixture looks like meal. With a fork, stir in milk until ingredients are just moistened, well blended, and cohesive. Pat into the prepared pan.

Bake until golden brown, 15 to 20 minutes. Then while still warm, split shortcake and spread lightly with *¼ cup butter;* fill and top with sweetened berries. Serve warm with light cream spooned over the top or with a generous dollop of Sweetened Whipped Cream.

$\mathcal{E}$FFIE'S EASY-TO-MAKE STRAWBERRY-PRESERVE ROLL

makes 6 to 8 servings

EFFIE MADE STRAWBERRY PRESERVES late in May and in early June. She would fill 8-ounce jelly jars full of the heady, sweetened preserved berries—some mashed, some whole—screw on the lids, and set them in a cool, dark, dry cupboard, which protected the rich red color.

Then since the chickens were laying a bountiful supply of eggs and rich cream rose daily on the milk, she would invite the whole family over to share several of these delicious jelly rolls, liberally filled with preserves and generously topped with dollops of whipped cream.

¾ cup sifted cake flour
¾ teaspoon baking powder
¼ teaspoon salt
4 eggs
¾ cup granulated sugar
1 teaspoon lemon extract
1 cup Strawberry Preserves, more if
    you wish (recipe follows)

½ recipe Sweetened Whipped
    Cream (page 17)
About ⅔ cup powdered sugar, plus
    ⅓ cup more for dusting cake
    roll

Preheat oven to 400°F. Line a greased 10½ × 15 × 1-inch jelly-roll pan with waxed paper, and then grease the paper.

Into a small bowl sift flour. In a large bowl, combine baking powder, salt, and eggs. Set the bowl in a pan of hot water and beat the mixture with a rotary egg beater, adding granulated sugar gradually until the whole becomes thick and light-lemon color. Remove the bowl from the hot water and add lemon extract. Fold in flour, gently so as not to stir down the volume of the beaten eggs.

Pour the batter into the prepared pan, spreading it evenly over the pan. Bake until lightly done, and not very brown, about 15 minutes.

While the cake is baking, dust a clean, heavy dish towel with the *⅔ cup powdered sugar*.

When cake is done, remove from oven and turn out onto the prepared dish towel. Take hold of the overhanging edges of the waxed paper, and gently shake the paper loose, peeling it off; trim away crisp edges of the cake. Starting from narrow end, roll up the cake in the towel; unroll it, and let it rest for a few minutes. Then reroll it in the towel and let it cool completely.

JANE WATSON HOPPING

When cooled, unroll the cake and spread surface with strawberry preserves. Reroll the cake and place on a serving platter, seam-side down. Dust with remaining *⅓ cup powdered sugar*. Slice thin and top, if you like, with a generous dollop of whipped cream.

$\mathcal{S}$TRAWBERRY PRESERVES

yield varies

WEIGH OUT 1 POUND OF SUGAR for each pound of strawberries. Put sugar in a large pot. Add half as much water as sugar. Cook to a thick syrup (224°F). Put the whole ripe fruit into the syrup and boil up just once. Pour onto earthenware plates and cover with glass. Set in the hottest sun for three days, taking the fruit in at night. The natural heat draws out the flavor better than boiling, and the fruit holds its shape perfectly. Put in jars and seal; simmer in a boiling-water bath for 15 minutes to kill mold spores. Store in a cool dark place.

THE COUNTRY MOTHERS COOKBOOK

AUNT IRENE'S FRESH STRAWBERRY SHERBET WITH ALMOND CLUSTER COOKIES

makes 2½ to 3 quarts sherbet

EVEN BEFORE SUMMER WAS officially at hand, our uncles unpacked the wooden hand-crank freezer, and on any day that was hot enough, made sherbet out of fragrant ripe strawberries. Sometimes the sherbet was made with milk, and sometime without. It was almost always served with Almond Cluster Cookies (recipe follows).

2 quarts ripe strawberries, hulled
2 cups sugar
¼ teaspoon salt

Juice of 2 lemons
Juice of 2 oranges
2 cups (1 pint) light cream

Assemble everything needed for freezing the sherbet before making the strawberry mixture. (See Churning Instructions, which follow.)

In a large bowl, crush berries with sugar. Set aside to blend for 30 minutes. Then strain sweetened berries through a fine sieve and chill. When thoroughly chilled, add salt, lemon and orange juices, and the cream. Pour into prepared crank-type freezer and freeze until firm.

JANE WATSON HOPPING

CHURNING INSTRUCTIONS

TO MAKE HOME-CHURNED SHERBET, begin by checking the equipment. Carefully wash the can and dasher in hot soapy water and rinse. Allow them to cool thoroughly. Then prepare the sherbet recipe as directed.

Crack the ice and determine its weight (if it isn't already weighed). When making a 4-quart freezer can of sherbet, use about *20 pounds of crushed ice,* and about *2½ cups rock salt.* If using *table salt,* use *1½ cups.*

Fill the freezer can only one-half to three-fourths full of the chilled sherbet mixture. (Don't overfill or the texture of the sherbet will suffer.) Set the can into the freezer pail and insert the dasher. Be sure the can is centered on the pivot in the bottom of the pail and that the dasher is correctly in place. Put the lid securely on the can; set the hand-crank unit in place over the top of the dasher and lock it in place.

To pack with ice and salt, first fill the bucket about one-third full of ice, sprinkle with salt, then add ice and salt in layers until the pail is full. More salt and ice may have to be added during the freezing period. After the bucket is full, wait 3 to 4 minutes before starting to churn.

When using a hand-crank freezer, turn slowly at first until a pull is felt, then triple the speed for about 5 to 10 minutes. About 20 minutes of steady cranking will freeze the sherbet to the consistency of mush. For immediate use, churn until sherbet is a little harder, 5 to 10 minutes more.

If the sherbet freezes too quickly (if the crank is difficult to turn after a very short time), this means too much salt has been added. A solid frozen layer has formed on the inside wall of the can, leaving the center unfrozen. To correct the situation, take the freezer apart, remove the dasher, and stir the frozen sherbet back down into the unfrozen mixture. Then, put the dasher back in place and reassemble the freezer. Remove the salt and ice from the bucket and repack with the correct proportions of ice and salt. Now you are ready to start churning again. Be certain that the drain hole is clear.

To open the freezer can, clean the salt and ice away from its top, pour off the salt water from the bucket, and wipe off the lid. Carefully remove the lid and take the dasher out, being careful not to get any salt water in the sherbet. Scrape the sherbet down from the side of the can and serve. When not serving out of the can, carefully replace clean lid. Unsalted ice may be packed in around the can to prevent meltage during the serving period.

$\mathcal{A}$LMOND CLUSTER COOKIES

makes about 3 dozen cookies

1 cup butter or margarine, softened
    at room temperature
4 tablespoons powdered sugar, plus
    about ⅔ cup for dusting cookies

1 teaspoon lemon extract
2 cups sifted all-purpose flour
2 cups slivered almonds

Preheat oven to 350°F. Set out a large ungreased cookie sheet.

In a large bowl, cream butter. Add *4 tablespoons powdered sugar* and continue beating until light. Blend in the lemon extract. Turn flour into the mixture and stir until well blended, then fold in almonds. Shape dough into small balls; place them about 1½ inches apart on the cookie sheet.

Bake until puffed, lightly browned, and firm to the touch, about 15 to 18 minutes. Remove from oven and while still hot roll in the *⅔ cup powdered sugar*. Lay out on brown paper to cool. When thoroughly cooled, store in an airtight tin or a glass jar with a tight-fitting lid.

THE BOOK OF JOYOUS CHILDREN

BOUND and bordered in leaf green,
  Edged with trellised buds and flowers
And glad Summer-gold, with clean
    White and purple morning-glories
    Such as suit the songs and stories
  Of this book of ours,
Unrevised in text or scene,—
    The Book of Joyous Children.

Wild and breathless in their glee—
  Lawless rangers of all ways
Winding through lush greenery
    Of Elysian vales—the viny,
    Bowery groves of shady, shiny
  Haunts of childish days.
Spread and read again with me
    The Book of Joyous Children.

What a whir of wings, and what
  Sudden drench of dews upon
The young brows, wreathed, all unsought,
    With the apple-blossom garlands
    Of the poets of those far lands
  When all dreams are drawn
Set herein and soiling not
    The Book of Joyous Children.

In their blithe companionship
  Taste again, these pages through,
The hot honey on your lip
    Of the sun-smit wild strawberry,
    Or the chill tart of the cherry;
  Kneel, all glowing, to
The cool spring, and with it sip
    The Book of Joyous Children.

As their laughter needs no rule,
  So accept their language, pray.—
Touch it not with any tool:
    Surely we may understand it,—
    As the heart has parsed or scanned it
  Is a worthy way,
Though found not in any School
    The Book of Joyous Children.

Be a truant—know no place
  Of prison under heaven's rim!
Front the Father's smiling face—
    Smiling, that *you* smile the brighter
    For the heavy hearts made lighter,
  Since you smile with Him.
Take—and thank Him for His grace—
    The Book of Joyous Children.

—James Whitcomb Riley

JANE WATSON HOPPING

Month of Roses, Month of Bees, and Month of Brides

IN JUNE, WHEN THE blossoms fall to be replaced by tiny green fruit, promising a good harvest, and summer, lush and verdant, begins to mature, roses splash riots of color across the landscape.

Cultivated roses display their elegance in stately hedges, and wild roses bloom abundantly along stream banks, skitter down cliff sides, and cling precariously on precipices, greeting the sun with small, delicate, single-petaled pink blossoms, and wantonly scatter their wild beauty over hillsides.

Amid the roses and about the other nectar-bearing flowers, bees hum and scurry, hesitating here and there to gather nature's sweet drink, only to rush back to the hive to layer them in, and thus produce the most fragrant and flavorful honey of the season.

For generations, this balmy month of sweethearts, richly colored and pregnant with natural bounty, has been acclaimed the most auspicious month for nuptials. Those performed while the moon is full have been thought especially blessed. Through the years, therefore, uneasy grooms and tender brides, wearing lustrous pearls—June's favored gem—have pledged their troth in June, and families and friends have rejoiced to witness the traditional rites observed celebrating a new union with loud rejoicing.

From FOR THE YOUNG

A Chapel, like a wild-bird's nest,
Closely embowered and trimly drest;
And thither young and old repair,
This Sabbath-day, for praise and prayer.

—William Wordsworth

Now the Sun Is Shining, and There Are Roses Everywhere

From THE LOVELY CHILD

LILIES are both pure and fair,
Growing 'midst the roses there—
Roses, too, both red and pink,
Are quite beautiful, I think.

But of all bright blossoms—best—
Purest—fairest—loveliest, —
Could there be a sweeter thing
Than a primrose, blossoming?

—James Whitcomb Riley

Effie was a romantic—so Mother said—who loved flowers more than most. Hers were labeled, and she kept a diary in which she jotted down their dates of blooming. But most fascinating to us, when we were young, were the stories she knew about roses.

When we walked alone with her in the rose garden, she told us all sorts of things. She would say: If you girls ever want to find out if a beau loves you, take a fresh-folded rose petal and strike it sharply against your forehead. If the petal cracks, the person in mind loves you; if not your love is not returned.

As she picked a bouquet of roses for us to take home to Mother, she would tell us that when a young man gave us a bouquet of roses that were still in the bud stage, it meant he thought that we were young and lovely; if he picked us a bouquet of wild roses, he was vowing eternal love. And she warned us about such men!

And as she gave us the flowers wrapped in a piece of waxed paper, so the thorns wouldn't scratch us, she would tuck in a sprig of rosemary for remembrance.

JANE WATSON HOPPING

ROSE-BLOSSOM TEA

THIS TEA IS MADE from dried petals (red preferred) and the tender leaves of fragrant varieties of roses. When mixed with lemon peel and lemon mint or other sweet herbs, it makes a delightful tea.

1 part pulverized dried rose petals   ½ part crushed cinnamon bark
½ part tender rose leaves
1 part mixed dried orange and
      lemon rinds

Keep this mixture in a jar with a tight lid. When making tea use *1 teaspoon tea* to *1 cup water*.

DRIED ROSEBUDS

OUR FAMILY'S FAVORITE FLOWERS for drying are miniature roses with names like Cupcake, glorious in shades of pink; Red Cascade; Party Girl, in creamy apricot flushed with salmon pink; or American Independence, in various shades of pink. Almost nothing is more lovely than the dainty flowers of the Cecile Brunner-Sweetheart Rose; the Sea Foam, which yields abundant foamy masses of pure white, teardrop-shaped buds that open into 2- to 3-inch cream-colored flowers. And the Fairy, at Mother's front door, with its graceful clusters of pink rosette blossoms that bloomed from early summer until hard frost.

All through the blooming season we pick barely unfurled buds, trim some of the older leaves from the stem, and leave tender young leaves to dry with the blossom. When trimmed, we bunch two or three stems together, fasten them with a wire twist or rubber band, and hang them upside down in an airy, shady spot—which protects the color and fragrance while they are drying.

When the blossoms are dry, we wrap them in sheets of waxed paper (florist paper is also excellent for this use), then gently lay them in a box or drawer from which light can be excluded, until we need them.

Made into large and small bouquets, rosebuds combined with baby's breath brighten the house throughout the winter months.

ROSE-PETAL VINEGAR

EFFIE LOVED NOT ONLY the scent of flowers but also the flavor. She had in her rose bed a large old-fashioned rose called Madame Isaac Pierre that was nearly eight feet tall, and which bore large quartered blooms with rolled petals of an intense rose-madder, large dark green leaves, and a rich raspberry aroma.

1 pint fragrant rose petals
1 quart white vinegar (Effie used
   cider vinegar, which was not
   nearly as nice as the white)

1 or 2 drops essence of roses (oil
   extract) which may be
   purchased at food specialty
   shops

Pick the newly opened roses in the morning before the heat and sunlight diminish the oils that yield both fragrance and flavor. Dip quickly in running cold water. Pull the petals off the rose and arrange them in a glass bottle. Pour cold vinegar, to which essence of roses has been added, over the petals until the bottle is filled. Stop with a cork. Set in a dry, cool dark place to mellow.

JANE WATSON HOPPING

As Good a Gyrl as Parent Ever Found!

CHILDREN, I'VE BEEN TOLD, don't really belong to us, they are only ours on loan from God. And I know that it must be true as I watch my own children, growing up and away, doing fine and making me so proud of them. And like mothers the world over, I take fierce pleasure in the fact that our loving bond is strong enough to bring them back home to share themselves and their lives with us.

Nothin' to Say, My Dear, Nothin' to Say

NOTHIN' TO SAY

SHE left you her little Bible—writ yer name acrost the page—
And left her ear bobs fer you, ef ever you come of age.
I've allus kep' 'em and gyuarded 'em, but ef yer goin' away—
Nothin' to say, my daughter! Nothin' at all to say!

You don't rikollect her, I reckon? No; you wasn't a year old then!
And now yer—how old *air* you? W'y, child, not *"twenty!"* When?
And yer nex' birthday's in Aprile? and you want to git married that day?
. . . I wisht yer mother was livin'!—But—I hain't got nothin' to say!

Twenty year! and as good a gyrl as parent ever found!
There's a straw ketched onto yer dress there—I'll bresh it off—turn round.
(Her mother was jes' twenty when us two run away!)
Nothin' to say, my daughter! Nothin' at all to say!

—James Whitcomb Riley

JANE WATSON HOPPING

AN OLD-FASHIONED ONE-TWO-THREE-FOUR CAKE WITH LEMON FILLING AND WHIPPED SNOW FROSTING

makes one 9-inch three-layer cake

THIS DELICIOUS CAKE HAS been served at many a birthday party, baby shower, and wedding in our family. It's one of the good old-time three-layer cakes that menfolk have loved through the generations, cutting great slices of it and washing it down with steaming coffee.

3 cups sifted cake flour
1 tablespoon baking powder
¼ teaspoon salt
1 cup butter or margarine, softened
   at room temperature
2 cups sugar

4 eggs, separated
1 cup milk
1 teaspoon vanilla extract
Lemon Filling (recipe follows)
Whipped Snow Frosting (recipe
   follows)

Preheat oven to 360°F. Grease three round 9-inch layer-cake pans; line with waxed paper and grease the paper; set aside.

Into a medium bowl, sift flour with baking powder and salt; set aside. In a large bowl, cream butter and sugar until light. Add egg yolks, beating well after each addition. Combine milk and vanilla. Alternately add flour and milk to the butter mixture, beating smooth after each addition. Then fold in *stiffly beaten egg whites*. Pour into prepared pans and bake until well risen and light golden brown, about 25 to 30 minutes. To test, insert a toothpick into the center of one layer; if it comes out clean the cake is done.

When cake is done, remove from oven and let set about 5 minutes; then turn layers out onto wire racks to cool. Remove waxed paper from the bottoms of the layers while they are still warm, but not hot. Turn right side up to cool. When the layers are thoroughly cooled, fill with Lemon Filling and frost with Whipped Snow Frosting.

$\mathscr{L}$EMON FILLING

makes enough filling to lightly fill one 3-layer cake

2 tablespoons all-purpose flour
¾ cup cold water
½ cup sugar
Grated rind of 1 lemon

1 tablespoon butter or margarine
Juice of 1 lemon, strained
1 egg yolk, beaten to a froth

In a small bowl, combine flour and *2 tablespoons water* into a smooth paste. Pour *remaining water* into a medium saucepan and add sugar, grated rind, and butter. Place over medium heat, stirring constantly. Cook until sugar is dissolved and mixture is boiling. Slowly stir in the flour paste and continue cooking and stirring until filling is clear and smooth, about 15 minutes. Then add the lemon juice and beaten egg yolk. Cook 2 minutes more. Cool thoroughly before spreading on cake (warm filling will soak into the cake).

$\mathscr{W}$HIPPED SNOW FROSTING

makes enough frosting to generously cover one 3-layer cake

1½ cups light corn syrup
4 egg whites

½ teaspoon salt
1 teaspoon vanilla extract

In a medium saucepan, heat corn syrup to the boiling point. In a large bowl, beat egg whites until stiff but not dry. Beat in salt. Slowly pour hot syrup over egg whites, beating constantly until the frosting is light and soft peaks form. Fold in vanilla.

About a Noble Race of Fairies

ON LONG WINTER EVENINGS, when rain poured down on our roof, Mother told us stories about fairies, tiny imaginary folk who loved to play tricks on real people, or who, when the urge struck, helped humans in time of need, sometimes with magic—not very strong magic, *jist a teeny bit.*

Our favorite story was about a noble race of fairies of the very highest kind, ruled over by tiny King Oberon and Queen Mab, whose court was made up of little lords and ladies. Robin Goodfellow or Puck, as he was often called, was the king's chief messenger and jester extraordinaire. He made everyone laugh and by his merry tricks kept life at court exciting. Queen Mab's little knight Pigwiggen loved her dearly and looked after her safety.

Like any real king, King Oberon had a mighty army—*well, not a real mighty army,* for none of his warriors were ever over a foot high; most of them were only six inches high, and some were even smaller than that. But they were very impressive to look at since all of them had glittering, pearly wings like those of large butterflies. Their gossamer bodies and wings were so thin and delicate that light could shine through them, enough so that they gleamed at night, twinkling like fireflies as they flew about.

Of old, it was rumored that the walls of King Oberon's palace were made of spiders' legs, the windows of cats' eyes, the roof of bats' wings painted with moonlight. His table was a mushroom, and he drank dew drops out of an acorn cup. Puck fanned him with a butterfly wing.

His Greatness, His Magnificence, His Wonderment—King Oberon moved his court from country to country, settling down near forest streams far from settled areas, staying longest in lands where poetry was written about himself or his subjects. And when the moon was full, he and his fairy court would join hands and dance all night inside a fairy ring of mushrooms, freshly popped out of the ground, or a circle of dark green which could be seen on the meadow grass.

Fairy tales, Mother would say, are ancient tales from long before stories were ever written down in books. Now and again, she would take us out to the fields to see with our very own eyes a bright green fairy ring, dancing all on its own with sunlight in the morning dew.

PUCK

O IT was Puck! I saw him yesternight
Swung up betwixt a phlox-top and the rim
   Of a low crescent moon that cradled him,
Whirring his rakish wings with all his might,
And pursing his wee mouth, that dimpled white
     And red, as though some dagger keen and slim
     Had stung him there, while ever faint and dim
His eery warblings piped his high delight:
Till I, grown jubilant, shrill answer made,
    At which all suddenly he dropped from view;
And peering after, 'neath the everglade,
    What was it, do you think, I saw him do?
I saw him peeling dewdrops with a blade
    Of starshine sharpened on his bat-wing shoe.

—James Whitcomb Riley

JANE WATSON HOPPING

ℱAIRY-LIGHT MERINGUES FILLED WITH SLIVERED ALMONDS

makes 12 to 15 meringues

EFFIE LOVED ANYTHING THAT was light, airy, and fancy, and she loved to surprise us all, especially her husband, Bud.

4 egg whites
¼ teaspoon cream of tartar
Dash of salt

1 cup sugar
1 teaspoon vanilla extract
⅔ cup slivered almonds

Preheat oven to 275°F. Cover a large cookie sheet with ungreased heavy brown paper.

Beat egg whites with cream of tartar and salt until they are stiff but not dry. Add sugar *1 tablespoonful* at a time, beating well after each addition. Fold in vanilla and slivered almonds. Drop meringue from a teaspoon or tablespoon onto the prepared cookie sheet.

Bake until lightly browned, 50 to 60 minutes. Remove from oven and take the meringues off of the pan immediately. Cool before serving.

LITTLE BROWNIES' MACAROONS FILLED WITH FLAKED COCONUT

makes 25 to 30 macaroons

ALL OF OUR LITTLE brownies loved to play in the backyard, in the rose garden, and under the trees and in them. When they came in, face and hands stained with play, they thought nothing was better with a glass of icy milk than chocolate macaroons filled with coconut.

4 egg whites
¼ cup water
⅔ cup sugar
2 teaspoons vanilla extract
1 tablespoon all-purpose flour

½ teaspoon salt
2 squares (2 ounces) unsweetened chocolate, melted
2½ cups flaked coconut

Preheat oven to 325°F. Cover a large cookie sheet with ungreased heavy brown paper.

Beat egg whites with water until they are stiff but not dry. Beat in sugar and vanilla. Combine flour and salt, folding in carefully. Then fold in melted chocolate and coconut. Drop from a teaspoon onto the prepared cookie sheet. Bake until light brown, 25 to 30 minutes.

JANE WATSON HOPPING

Drowsy Old Summer

SUMMER, WHICH BEGINS WITH tender blossoms and lush green grasses and herbs, reaches its peak in the hot, dry month of July. Then, as the air becomes clear and the sun scorching, the greenness of June fades into burned yellows and tans. Oddly, the droughty weather brings out brilliant colors in summer annuals like sweet peas, cosmos, petunias, snapdragons, and zinnias. Gardens thrive, fruits and berries sweeten and ripen in the heat.

Out in heavily grazed pastures, cattle find deep shade in which they stand, barely moving, or lie against the cooler earth, switching pesky flies off their hides. Humans, too, seek relief.

BEST OF ALL

OF all good gifts that the Lord lets fall,
Is not silence the best of all?

The deep, sweet hush when the song is closed,
And every sound but a voiceless ghost;

And every sigh, as we listening leant,
A breathless quiet of vast content?

The laughs we laughed have a purer ring
With but their memory echoing;

And the joys we voiced, and the words we said,
Seem so dearer for being dead.

So of all good gifts that the Lord lets fall,
Is not silence the best of all?

—James Whitcomb Riley

JANE WATSON HOPPING

Blessed Are They
Who Sing in the Morning

AFTER I WAS MARRIED, I loved to stay overnight with Raymond's grandmother, Grandma White. She mothered me, telling me to wash my face and hands in cold water before breakfast so that I would be bright and shiny to meet the morning. She was cheerful and industrious, faced her problems with energy and courage, and to the very end she took joy out of life. I loved her, was inspired by her, and remember her every day:

WHEN EVENING SHADOWS FALL

WHEN evening shadows fall,
 She hangs her cares away
Like empty garments on the wall
 That hides her from the day;
And while old memories throng,
 And vanished voices call,
She lifts her grateful heart in song
 When evening shadows fall.

Her weary hands forget
 The burdens of the day.
The weight of sorrow and regret
 In music rolls away;
And from the day's dull tomb,
 That holds her in its thrall,
Her soul springs up in lily bloom
 When evening shadows fall.

O weary heart and hand,
 Go bravely to the strife—
No victory is half so grand
 As that which conquers life!

—James Whitcomb Riley

THE COUNTRY MOTHERS COOKBOOK

JANE WATSON HOPPING

*E*XTRA-SPECIAL RHUBARB PIE

makes one 9-inch pie

RHUBARB PLANTS OFTEN STAND three feet high, with large deep green leaves; the stalks, red or pink in color, are pulled from the plant, not cut or broken off. Auntie told young gardeners who admired her rhubarb that the stalks should always be picked when they were firm and tender, as older stalks became stringy and lost the lovely crisp flavor for which the plant was famous. She also warned that since the leaves contain oxalic acid, they are poisonous to humans and to livestock.

Double-Crust Pastry (recipe follows)
1½ cups sugar
⅓ cup all-purpose flour
Pinch of salt (⅛ teaspoon)
½ teaspoon vanilla (an old-time
　　secret ingredient for this kind of
　　pie)

5 cups cut rhubarb (cut into ½-inch
　　pieces)
2 to 3 tablespoons butter or
　　margarine, as desired

Make pastry, wrap it in waxed paper or foil, and chill before preparing the filling. Preheat oven to 450°F. Set out a 9-inch pie pan.

Remove pastry from refrigerator and cut approximately in half. Roll out one half on a lightly floured surface. Fold dough in half and line pie pan, making a bottom crust (don't trim at this point). Roll out second half of dough; fold it in half and then into quarters, sprinkling lightly with flour as you fold.

In a large bowl, combine sugar, flour, salt, and vanilla and stir to mix well. Add rhubarb and toss until well coated. Pile filling into the lined pan, then dot fruit with butter. Moisten the edge of the bottom crust and arrange the top crust over the filling. Trim excess dough, leaving about 1-inch overhang. Turn overhang under the bottom crust, which leaves a generous edging. Crimp between thumb and forefingers. Cut vents in the top for steam to escape.

Bake pie in 450°F oven for 15 minutes to set crust; then turn down heat to 350°F and continue baking for 35 to 40 minutes longer. Serve while slightly warm, plain or with ice cream.

DOUBLE-CRUST PASTRY

makes pastry for one 9-inch pie

2 cups all-purpose flour, plus flour
    for rolling out dough
1 teaspoon salt

¾ cup cold butter or margarine
1¼ cup cold water

In a medium-size bowl, combine the flour and salt. Cut in the butter until the mixture resembles grains of corn. Sprinkle the water over the mixture and mix thoroughly with a fork until all particles cling together to form a ball. Chill until needed.

EASY-TO-MAKE EARLY-PEACH BUTTER

SWEETENED WITH CLOVER HONEY, this peach butter, from the first fruits of the season was a real treat when spread over Grandma's piping hot Deluxe Muffins (page 157).

2 cups peeled, pitted, and ground
    peaches

1 cup honey

Put peaches and honey in a heavy-bottomed saucepan, bring to a boil, then turn down heat to medium and cook until quite thick, for about 1 hour, stirring frequently. When thick, ladle into sterilized half-pint canning jars. Seal with thoroughly washed and sterilized lids and rings. Set aside to cool. When cool, check the lid—it should be concave.

NOTE: If you make more than a small batch for immediate use, simmer the filled sealed jars for about 15 minutes in a boiling-water bath; cool, then store.

GRANDMA'S DELUXE MUFFINS

makes 12 medium muffins

WHEN MAKING THESE MUFFINS, Grandma always cut the butter into the flour mixture as one would cut shortening into biscuits or pie crust rather than adding melted butter along with the eggs and milk. Grandma's method prevents over-stirring, which tends to make muffins heavy and doughy. Her never-fail method yielded a fine, light-textured muffin, whether the recipe was made by an experienced cook or by a young girl.

2 cups sifted all-purpose flour
2½ teaspoons baking powder
4 tablespoons sugar
¾ teaspoon salt

½ cup cold butter or margarine
1 egg, well beaten
¾ cup milk

Preheat oven to 400°F. Grease a 12-cup muffin tin that has medium cups.

Into a large bowl, sift flour with baking powder, sugar, and salt. With a pastry blender, cut in butter. Then combine egg and milk. Add all at once to flour mixture. Draw a spoon through the batter, from the side of the bowl toward the center, several times, turning the bowl gradually. Then draw the spoon through the batter several times more. Stir only until all dry ingredients are dampened.

Turn into prepared muffin cups; fill each about two-thirds full. Bake until well risen, light brown, and firm to the touch, about 25 minutes. Remove from oven and serve piping hot with or without peach butter.

Cherries, Harbingers of Summer

WE HAVE A CHERRY tree in our front yard that is as tall as our story-and-a-half house. The trunk is so large and the canopy so wide that everyone who sees it in gloriously full bloom speculates about its age, and wonders if it had been planted a hundred-plus years ago when the house was first built. The cherries on it are golden with a red blush, a bit tart even though the tree bears sweet cherries, not pie cherries.

In spring I stand at the upstairs bedroom window and bask in the thickly clustered cloud of blossoms. In summer I pick a few of the first ripe cherries and immediately eat them out of hand. Later, when the boughs are heavy with ripe fruit, I am awakened in the night to the sound of raccoons high up in the tree, fighting over the cherries. In moments, our awakened family crowds about the window and we watch the varmints clinging to the tree limbs, following the beam of our flashlight with their eyes. They are as curious and amazed watching our antics as we are watching theirs.

From BILLY BOY

OH, where have you been, Billy Boy, Billy Boy,
Oh, where have you been, charming Billy?
I have been to seek a wife,
She's the joy of my life,
She's a young thing and cannot leave her mother.

Did she bid you to come in, Billy Boy, Billy Boy,
Did she bid you to come in, charming Billy?
Yes she bade me to come in,
There's a dimple in her chin,
She's a young thing and cannot leave her mother.

Can she bake a cherry pie, Billy Boy, Billy Boy,
Can she bake a cherry pie, charming Billy?
She can bake a cherry pie,
Quick as a cat can wink it's eye,
She's a young thing and cannot leave her mother.

—Edward L. White

JANE WATSON HOPPING

158

$\mathscr{A}$ SIMPLE OLD-TIME CHERRY PIE

makes one 9-inch cherry pie

ADA'S EASY-TO-MAKE fresh Bing cherry pie was always a hit with the men in the family, who usually spooned thick cream over generous servings. On hot July evenings they would offer to churn homemade vanilla ice cream to go with the pie.

Double-Crust Pastry (page 156)
2½ cups cherries, pitted and
    drained (reserve juice)
1 cup sugar, plus 3 tablespoons for
    sprinkling over pie before
    baking
2 tablespoons minute tapioca
⅛ teaspoon salt

1 tablespoon butter or margarine,
    melted
1 cup cherry juice, add water if
    necessary
1 teaspoon cornstarch
¼ cup light or heavy cream for
    glazing top crust

Make crust, roll out bottom portion, and line a 9-inch pie pan before preparing the filling. Also, roll out top crust, dust with flour, fold in quarters, and cover with a piece of waxed paper. Preheat oven to 425°F.

In a medium bowl, combine cherries, *1 cup sugar,* tapioca, salt, butter, cherry juice, and cornstarch. Let stand 15 minutes, then pour filling into the prepared pie pan. Moisten pastry edge with water and cover with prepared top crust. Crimp edges and with a knife, slit top crust to permit steam to escape. Then spread a thin coating of cream over the crust and sprinkle with *3 table-spoons* sugar.

Bake until crust is nicely browned and filling is bubbling up, about 45 minutes. Remove from oven and set on a wire rack to cool. When pie has cooled to room temperature, serve with or without topping.

Old-Fashioned Homemade Maraschino Cherries

makes about 6 pints

EFFIE THOUGHT THESE SWEET, almond-flavored maraschino cherries could be made with either deep-red Bing or light-colored Royal Anne cherries.

5 pounds sweet cherries, pitted

4 pounds sugar

2 teaspoons red food coloring

4 teaspoons almond extract

1 tablespoon lemon juice

Put cherries and sugar into a large saucepan, stir gently until juices begin to form, and cook slowly until thick. Remove from heat and add food coloring, almond extract, and lemon juice. Cook 10 to 15 minutes longer, then pack hot in sterilized jars. Seal with sterilized lids and rings. Process in boiling-water bath 20 minutes. Cool, test the seal (the jars are completely sealed if the lid is concave), store in a cool dark place to preserve the rich color.

CHERRY RIPE

ROBINS in the cherry-tree—
Come on and get a pail!

From white to green,
  From green to red,
  The cherries ripen overhead,
  Until a luscious feast is spread
For all who dare to climb,
And every hungry bird has seen
  That it is dinner-time.

Robins in the cherry-tree—
Who'll help to fill the pail?

—Walter Prichard Eaton

JANE WATSON HOPPING

Borne on Its Native Breezes

EARLY IN 1917, ONLY two weeks after his mother had died, Uncle Arch, a gentle boy just turned twenty-one, was drafted into the army and sent to France, where he served in the medical corps. He was the child in Mother's family who never hurt anyone or anything; he was the child who hid out on butchering day.

The night he came home from the "war to end all wars," his German neighbors, all farmers, came over to talk to him about his time in France, eager to know, eager to ask if he had learned anything about their families still in Germany, asking if the price had been too high. They were the good country neighbors of his childhood, the people who had been so kind to him and to his family when his mother had died. He talked with them for hours, answering their questions the best he could, quietly, easing fears for loved ones whenever he could.

After the neighbors went home, and his duty to them was done, he never mentioned the war again.

*A*UNT FANNY'S LIBERTY CAKE WITH LEMON ICING

makes one 8-inch three-layer cake

AUNTIE LOVED TO MAKE this cake for the Fourth of July. She named it herself, frosted it with a Lemon Icing, and stuck minature flags and red candles all over the top of the cake. Auntie served her patriotic cake with hot coffee after the fathers and uncles shot off all of the fireworks.

One year she made us all sing "The Star-Spangled Banner" and "God Bless America" while the rockets lit the sky. Then she hugged and kissed all of us children and told us never to forget what it means to be free.

1 cup butter or margarine, softened at room temperature	1 cup buttermilk
	½ teaspoon lemon extract
1½ cups sugar, plus ⅔ cup for combining with egg whites	½ teaspoon almond extract
	6 egg whites
3 cups sifted cake flour	1 teaspoon cream of tartar
½ teaspoon salt	Lemon Icing (recipe follows)
1 teaspoon baking soda	

Preheat oven to 375°F. Grease and flour three round 8-inch layer-cake pans. Set aside.

In a large bowl, cream butter; gradually add *1½ cups sugar* and cream until light. Sift flour with salt and baking soda. Combine buttermilk with lemon and almond extracts. Then alternately add sifted flour mixture in thirds with buttermilk mixture. Beat well after each addition. In a second large bowl, beat egg whites until frothy; add cream of tartar and remaining *⅔ cup sugar* gradually, and continue beating until egg whites are stiff but not dry. Fold butter-flour mixture into beaten egg whites, working carefully so as not to lessen the volume of egg whites.

Turn into prepared pans. Bake until well risen, light brown, and firm to the touch, about 30 minutes. Remove from oven, let cool 10 minutes, then turn out of the pans onto wire rack to cool. When thoroughly cooled, fill and frost with Lemon Icing.

$\mathcal{L}$EMON ICING

makes enough to fill and frost one 3-layer cake

3 cups sifted powdered sugar
2 tablespoons light cream, more if
    needed to make icing spread
    smoothly

1 tablespoon lemon juice, strained
½ teaspoon finely grated lemon
    peel

In a medium bowl, combine sugar and cream, beating until a moderately thick icing is formed. Add lemon juice and lemon peel; stir to blend. If needed, add just enough additional cream to thin icing so that it will spread thinly and evenly. Ice layers as you stack them together, and then lightly cover both top and side of the cake. Use immediately.

LIBERTY

SING! every bird, to-day!
  Sing for the sky so clear,
    And the gracious breath of the atmosphere
Shall waft our cares away.
Sing! sing! for the sunshine free;
Sing through the land from sea to sea;
Lift each voice in the highest key
    And sing for Liberty!

Sing for the arms that fling
  Their fetters in the dust
  And lift their hands in higher trust
Unto the one Great King;
Sing for the patriot heart and hand;
Sing for the country they have planned;
Sing that the world may understand
    This is Freedom's land!

Sing in the tones of prayer,
  Sing till the soaring soul
  Shall float above the world's control
In Freedom everywhere!
Sing for the good that is to be,
Sing for the eyes that are to see
The land where man at last is free,
    O sing for Liberty!

—James Whitcomb Riley

Childhood Paths Once More So Dear

UNCLE BUD HAS ALWAYS told us stories about his boyhood life in the woods and how he loved to wander alone in the wilderness in late July, or race about playing Indians in the woods with his brother Joe, his joy at seeing chipmunks, sudden-whirring quail, squirrels with silver tails and pheasants. As he grew older, his stories became more and more tender until the glossy light of tears waiting to fall sometimes stood in his eyes:

JANE WATSON HOPPING

From A SUMMER DAY

THE Summer's put the idy in
My head that I'm a boy ag'in;
And all around's so bright and gay
I want to put my team away,
And jest get out whare I can lay
And soak my hide full of the day!
But work is work, and must be done—
Yit, as I work, I have my fun,
Jest fancyin' these furries here
Is childhood's paths onc't more so dear—
And so I walk through medder-lands,
And country lanes, and swampy trails
Whare long bullrushes bresh my hands;
And, tilted on the ridered rails
Of deadnin' fences, "Old Bob White"
Wissels his name in high delight,
And whirs away. I wunder still,
Whichever way a boy's fee will—
Whare trees has fell, with tangled tops
Whare dead leaves shakes, I stop fer breth,
Heerin' the acon as it drops—
Histin' my chin up still as deth,
And watchin' clos't, with upturned eyes.

—James Whitcomb Riley

Good Old Summer Vittles

UNDER THE HOT SUMMER sun, squashes grow rapidly and abundantly until boxes of them, picked while small, medium, and large, clutter porches and storerooms. Every female member of the family plots ways to use them up.

Gardens are searched for table cucumbers and pickling cucumbers that are large enough for suppertime use. Young beets, both root and greens, are pulled for steaming; early Golden Acre cabbages, already too long in the field and about to burst in the heat, are trimmed and made immediately into slaw, cooked cabbage, or a jar or two of kraut. New potatoes can be grabbled out of their hills, and green beans, pencil-thin, half hidden under a canopy of leaves, promise a scant few for supper and a bounteous harvest, come August.

Along the creeks and in the pasture, wild blackberries are turning color and sweetening up; early apples, first baked into pies, then, as they ripen, eaten out of hand, hang thickly in the trees. Early peach varieties, just becoming sun ripened, are served in heirloom glass serving dishes swimming in cream.

Milk flows abundantly; chicken, rabbit, and fresh-caught fish grace farm tables at noon and at suppertime.

JANE WATSON HOPPING

ℰFFIE'S CRISPY BAKED CHICKEN

makes about 4 servings

FROM THE THIRTIES ON, Effie introduced us all to new twists on old ideas like this one. Needless to say, her crispy chicken was a hit with the menfolks, and the recipe passed from hand to hand.

3-pound frying chicken
1 cup skim milk (in old-time
    kitchens, the cream was
    religiously skimmed off the milk,
    to be used for other purposes
    than drinking)

1 cup cornflake crumbs
1 teaspoon dried oregano leaves,
    finely pulverized between thumb
    and fingers
¼ teaspoon salt
¼ teaspoon black pepper

Preheat oven to 400°F. Grease a 12 × 9–inch baking pan. Set aside.

Remove all excess fat from chicken, particularly that which lies in the body cavity (also fatty pieces of skin, if you wish), then cut into serving pieces. Rinse and dry the meat thoroughly. Dip in milk, then in cornflake crumbs which have been thoroughly combined with oregano, salt, and pepper. Let stand so that coating will adhere.

Place chicken in the prepared baking pan. Do not crowd; pieces should not touch. Bake until crumbs form a crisp skin, about 45 minutes.

$\mathcal{A}$UNT IRENE'S STEAMED BROOK TROUT

MANY SMALL WHOLE FISH are available in early summer, among them delicately flavored brook trout, which are delicious steamed. Auntie preferred this cooking method as it preserved the fresh-caught flavor. She thought only one kind of fish should be steamed at a time to keep the flavors pure.

To steam fish, a kettle with a perforated tray designed to keep the fish out of the water is needed. If you do not have one, set a colander over a kettle of boiling water. Salt and pepper the fish and cover the kettle tightly. Allow about 10 to 15 minutes cooking time per pound.

Two plates may also be used for steaming fish. Butter one plate and put fish on it; cover fish with a piece of well-buttered paper and invert the second plate over the first. Place the plates over a saucepan of boiling water and let fish steam for 20 to 30 minutes. The lower plate may be a pie tin with holes in it to let the steam surround the fish, but such a steamer, like the colander, lets the juices run out.

Serve steamed fish with butter and wedges of lemon.

$\mathcal{T}$ANG

makes 4 to 6 servings

THIS IS AN OLD southern recipe that was written on a piece of school paper and slipped into our old "doctor" book.

3 medium slices farm bacon
2 quarts thickly sliced summer
    squash (zucchini, patty pan, and
    yellow crookneck are of ancient
    origin)

Water to cover
1 teaspoon salt
¼ teaspoon pepper

In a large skillet, fry bacon until quite crisp, transfer to a platter to drain, and set aside in the warming oven. Set hot skillet with *3 tablespoons drippings* aside; discard the rest of the drippings.

Into a large saucepan, put the sliced summer squash. Barely cover with water and let simmer until the water is almost absorbed. Then season to taste with salt and pepper. Turn squash into skillet and fry in reserved bacon drippings to a light brown. Serve with bacon.

$\mathcal{L}$IGHT-GREEN COLESLAW

makes 4 to 6 servings

STONEHEAD CABBAGES ARE ROUND and rock-solid, so tightly packed with leaves that they're extra heavy for their size, weighing four to six and a half pounds each. These early cabbages are harvested in late spring and early summer. They are more resistant to splitting in hot weather than the older varieties.

½ small head of cabbage
3 tablespoons minced celery
4 tablespoons cider vinegar
1 tablespoon salad or olive oil
1 tablespoon sugar

1 teaspoon dry mustard
¼ teaspoon salt
Dash of black pepper
Parsley for garnish, optional

Chop or shred cabbage; add minced celery. In a small bowl, combine vinegar, oil, sugar, mustard, salt, and pepper. Pour over salad; toss well. Turn into a glass serving bowl and garnish with parsley, if you wish.

SHEILA'S SOUTHERN FRIED OKRA

makes 6 to 8 servings

LIKE CUCUMBERS AND ZUCCHINI, okra ages quickly; in the blink of an eye it grows beyond the tender, edible stage. Sheila, therefore, picks the pods when they are three to five days past flowering and about two to four inches long.

Oil or lard for deep-fat frying
2 to 4 pods okra per person
1 tablespoon water

1 egg, slightly beaten
Cornmeal for dipping
Salt and pepper to taste

Heat fat to 380°F for deep-fat frying (Mother heated it until it browned a crust of bread).

Wash okra pods thoroughly but don't soak. Cut off stems and then cut pods in half, lengthwise. Smaller pods may be cooked whole. Mix 1 tablespoon water into the slightly beaten egg and dip okra first in egg and then in cornmeal. Drop in the hot fat and brown until crisp. Salt and pepper lightly and serve warm.

AUNT FANNY'S LEMON CLOVERLEAF ROLLS GLAZED WITH HEAVY CREAM

makes 12 rolls

THESE DELICIOUS ROLLS ARE typical of Aunt Fanny's almost instant company fare. She usually set out a butter ball etched with the tines of a fork, and a fresh jar of whatever jam was in season.

2 cups sifted all-purpose flour
¾ teaspoon baking soda
½ teaspoon salt
¼ cup sugar
⅓ cup cold butter or margarine

½ cup milk
3 tablespoons lemon juice
About 3 tablespoons heavy cream, to glaze rolls

JANE WATSON HOPPING

Preheat oven to 450°F. Grease the cups of a 12-cup muffin tin.

Into a large bowl, sift flour with soda, salt, and sugar. Then with a pastry blender or the fingertips, cut or rub in the butter until flour mixture is texture of coarse cornmeal. Add combined milk and lemon juice, stirring quickly into a soft dough. Turn out onto a lightly floured surface and knead just enough to make the dough cohesive and easy to handle. Form into small balls about the size of a marble. Place three in each muffin cup.

Bake until rolls are golden brown, about 20 minutes. Remove from oven. To glaze: lightly wash tops of rolls with heavy cream. Serve piping hot.

GOOSEBERRY PIE

makes one 9-inch pie

UNCLE BEN LOVED GOOSEBERRY pie. He thought the berries should be left on the bush until they were yellow-tinted. He said the pie was then more flavorful and sweet.

¾ cup boiling water	6 tablespoons all-purpose flour
3 cups gooseberries	¼ teaspoon salt
1 cup sugar	Double-Crust Pie Pastry (page 156)

Preheat oven to 450°F. Pick over, wash, and drain gooseberries; set aside. Set out a 9-inch pie pan.

Into a medium saucepan, pour boiling water over berries; cook until tender. Meanwhile, in a small bowl, combine sugar, flour, and salt. When berries are tender, turn off the heat and stir in flour mixture, stirring constantly until blended. Let filling cool.

Meanwhile, prepare crust. Line a 9-inch pie pan with half the pastry; pour the cooled filling into the crust. Roll out the top crust and lay it over the filling; cut vent holes in the top; trim and crimp edge.

Bake in hot oven for 10 minutes; then at 350°F until crust is golden brown and filling is bubbling, about 35 minutes more.

Congo, Black Diamond, Rattlesnake, Ain't Them Purty Names fer Wortermelons?

GRANDPA NOT ONLY LOVED to eat watermelons but loved to grow them, too. Nothing pleased him more than to see them lying in the field, weighing thirty-five or forty pounds apiece. And when the neighbors all came over for a feed, that kind of socializing just couldn't be beat:

WORTERMELON TIME

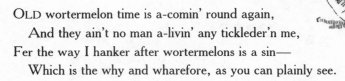

OLD wortermelon time is a-comin' round again,
    And they ain't no man a-livin' any tickleder'n me,
Fer the way I hanker after wortermelons is a sin—
    Which is the why and wharefore, as you can plainly see.

Oh! it's in the sandy soil wortermelons does the best,
    And it's thare they'll lay and waller in the sunshine and the dew
Tel they wear all the green streaks clean off of theyr breast;
    And you bet I ain't a-findin' any fault with them; air you?

They ain't no better thing in the vegetable line;
    And they don't need much 'tendin', as ev'ry farmer knows;
And when theyr ripe and ready fer to pluck from the vine,
    I want to say to you theyr the best fruit that grows.

It's some likes the yeller-core, and some likes the red,
    And it's some says "The Little Californy" is the best;
But the sweetest slice of all I ever wedged in my head,
    Is the old "Edingburg Mounting-sprout," of the west.

You don't want no punkins nigh your wortermelon vines—
    'Cause, some-way-another, they'll spile your melons, shore;—
I've seed 'em taste like punkins, from the core to the rines,
    Which may be a fact you have heerd of before.

JANE WATSON HOPPING

172

But your melons that's raised right and 'tended to with care,
    You can walk around amongst'em with a parent's pride and joy,
And thump 'em on the heads with as fatherly a air
    As ef each one of them was your little girl er boy.

I joy in my hart jest to hear that rippin' sound
    When you split one down the back and jolt the halves in two,
And the friends you love the best is gethered all around—
    And you says unto your sweethart, "Oh, here's the core fer you!"

And I like to slice 'em up in big pieces fer 'em all,
    Espeshally the children, and watch theyr high delight
As one by one the rines with theyr pink notches falls,
    And they holler fer some more, with unquenched appetite.

Boys takes to it natchurl, and I like to see 'em eat—
    A slice of wortermelon's like a frenchharp in theyr hands,
And when they "saw" it through theyr mouth sich music can't be beat—
    'Cause it's music both the sperit and the stummick understands.

Oh, they's more in wortermelons than the purty-colored meat,
    And the overflowin' sweetness of the worter squshed betwixt
The up'ard and the down'ard motions of a feller's teeth,
    And it's the taste of ripe old age and juicy childhood mixed.

Fer I never taste a melon but my thoughts flies away
    To the summertime of youth; and again I see the dawn,
And the fadin' afternoon of the long summer day,
    And the dusk and dew a-fallin', and the night a-comin' on.

And thare's the corn around us, and the lispin' leaves and trees,
    And the stars a-peekin' down on us as still as silver mice,
And us boys in the wortermelons on our hands and knees,
    And the new-moon hangin' ore us like a yeller-cored slice.

Oh! it's wortermelon time is a-coming' round again,
    And they ain't no man a-livin' any tickleder'n me,
Fer the way I hanker after wortermelons is a sin—
    Which is the why and wharefore, as you can plainly see.

             —James Whitcomb Riley

THE COUNTRY MOTHERS COOKBOOK

$\mathcal{A}$ FANCY WATERMELON SALAD WITH WHIPPED-CREAM MAYONNAISE

makes 6 or more servings

ABOUT 1932, EFFIE FOUND this recipe, which instantly became a family favorite. All of us thought it was delicious—except Grandpa, who more than once said that the women should leave the melons alone, just leave them natural "like they was suppose to be."

1 medium ripe watermelon	Lettuce leaves
¼ cup powdered sugar	Whipped-Cream Mayonnaise
1 quart ginger ale	(recipe follows)

Using a teaspoon (or melon-ball scoop) scoop out the pulp from watermelon. Drain off juices and put pulp in a large bowl. Sprinkle with sugar and cover with ginger ale. Refrigerate 30 minutes; then drain off the liquid, which may be served over ice as a beverage, reserving 2 tablespoons juice for Whipped-Cream Mayonnaise. Arrange the drained pulp in large lettuce-leaf cups for individual servings, or in a large leaf-lined serving bowl for table service. Top with a generous dollop of Whipped Cream Mayonnaise.

$\mathcal{W}$HIPPED-CREAM MAYONNAISE

makes enough topping for 6 or more servings

½ cup heavy cream	Pinch of salt
1 tablespoon powdered sugar	Dash of paprika
½ cup mayonnaise	
2 tablespoons watermelon juice,	
reserved from preceding recipe	

In a small bowl, whip cream until soft peaks form; stir in sugar. In a medium bowl, blend mayonnaise with watermelon juice, salt, and paprika. Fold in whipped cream.

JANE WATSON HOPPING

THE COUNTRY MOTHERS COOKBOOK

AUNT FANNY'S HAM SALAD IN A SCALLOPED WATERMELON BOAT WITH LEMON MAYONNAISE DRESSING

makes enough salad for 12 servings

NOT TO BE OUTDONE when it came to fancy melon dishes, Auntie began to fix this special salad for summertime family potlucks. We children thought it was the best thing we had ever eaten. For this salad she preferred a Rattlesnake melon, named for its light and dark green markings. Auntie thought the firm, bright, rose-colored flesh and super-sweet flavor was perfect for making melon balls, and that the pretty oblong shell was just the right shape for making a scalloped watermelon boat.

1 large watermelon
2 quarts cubed boiled ham
2 cups seedless green grapes
    (Thompson Seedless preferred)
2 cups seedless red grapes (Red
    Flame preferred)

3 cups diagonally sliced celery, use
    light-colored stalks
Lemon Mayonnaise Dressing (recipe
    follows)

Cut watermelon in half lengthwise, about 1 inch above the center. Using a melon-ball scoop or a teaspoon, remove flesh from each half of melon and gently put melon balls into a large bowl. When only bits of flesh remain, set the melon balls in the refrigerator to chill. Remove seeds and into a large bowl, scrape any remaining flesh. *Reserve the lower shell for making a scalloped boat.*

While melon balls chill, prepare watermelon boat. First measure the circumference of the rind, dividing the total so that it will yield scallops of equal size. Cut a cardboard pattern based on desired width of scallops. Trace pattern around top edge of rind. Using a small sharp knife, scallop the edge of the rind. Chill watermelon boat until serving time.

In a large bowl, combine ham cubes, green and red grapes, and celery. Fold in Lemon Mayonnaise Dressing. Cover and chill. Just before serving, spoon dressed ham mixture into the boat alternately with melon balls. Don't stir the melon into the other ingredients (the bright red melon balls are quite lovely if left uncoated or only partially coated with dressing). Serve immediately in generous serving bowls.

$\mathcal{L}$EMON MAYONNAISE DRESSING

makes about ½ cup dressing

½ cup mayonnaise
1 tablespoon lemon juice

2 tablespoons powdered sugar

Measure into a small bowl and stir to blend.

Long Purple Berries That Rained on the Ground

MULBERRY TREES ARE NAMED for the color of their fruit, white, red, and black. The Red Mulberry, our common American mulberry tree, grows from Massachusetts to Florida, and west to Kansas and Nebraska. It is the largest of the mulberry trees, growing to a height of sixty to seventy feet. The wood is medium-grained and strong, and is used for fence posts and the interior of homes.

Birds eagerly eat the purplish-red fruit, as do countryfolk, who make pies, preserves, and wine out of the mulberries. Some women prefer the shrubby white mulberries, which they say are sweeter than the purple variety. Country women with European backgrounds prefer the black varieties. Midwesterners like my neighbor recall childhood days, purple-stained mouths and hands, and the thickly hanging fruit, picked sweet and dead ripe.

THE MULBERRY TREE

O, IT'S many's the scenes which is dear to my mind
As I think of my childhood so long left behind;
The home of my birth, with its old puncheon-floor,
And the bright morning-glorys that growed round the door;
The warped clabboard roof whare the rain it run off
Into streams of sweet dreams as I laid in the loft,
Countin' all of the joys that was dearest to me,
And a-thinkin' the most of the mulberry tree.

And to-day as I dream, with both eyes wide-awake,
I can see the old tree, and its limbs as they shake,
And the long purple berries that rained on the ground
Whare the pastur' was bald whare we trommpt it around.
And again, peekin' up through the thick leafy shade,
I can see the glad smiles of the friends when I strayed
With my little bare feet from my own mother's knee
To foller them off to the mulberry tree.

Leanin' up in the forks, I can see the old rail,
And the boy climbin' up it, claw, tooth, and toe-nail,
And in fancy can hear, as he spits on his hands,
The ring of his laugh and the rip of his pants.
But that rail led to glory, as certain and shore
As I'll never climb thare by that rout' any more—
What was all the green lauruls of Fame unto me,
With my brows in the boughs of the mulberry tree!

Then it's who can fergit the old mulberry tree
That he knowed in the days when his thoughts was as free
As the flutterin' wings of the birds that flew out
Of the tall wavin' tops as the boys come about?
O, a crowd of my memories, laughin' and gay,
Is a-climbin' the fence of that pastur' to-day,
And a-pantin' with joy, as us boys ust to be,
They go racin' acrost fer the mulberry tree.

—James Whitcomb Riley

THE COUNTRY MOTHERS COOKBOOK

MULBERRY CRUNCH WITH AN OATMEAL TOPPING

makes 6 to 8 dessert servings

MULBERRIES, WHICH LOOK SOMEWHAT like a purplish-black loganberry, are about one or more inches long and grow on trees (not vines). Year after year such trees bear large crops of rich-flavored berries that are unbeatable for preserves, pies, or cobblers. We like them in this crunch.

1 cup granulated sugar
3 tablespoons all-purpose flour

4 cups mulberries, stemmed

Preheat oven to 350°F.

In a small bowl, combine granulated sugar and *3 tablespoons flour,* mixing well. Place mulberries in a large bowl and add the sugar and flour mixture, tossing until berries are coated. Place in a 9 × 9 × 2-inch pan or dish.

OATMEAL TOPPING
½ cup light brown sugar, firmly
   packed
½ cup dry quick-cooking oats

½ cup butter or margarine
⅓ cup all-purpose flour

TO MAKE OATMEAL TOPPING
In a small bowl, combine topping ingredients, stirring until mixture is crumbly. Sprinkle topping evenly over mulberry mixture. Bake 45 minutes. When done, mulberries are tender, juice is thick and bubbling, and topping is lightly browned and crusty.

The Plaint Human

Season of snows, and season of flowers,
  Seasons of loss and gain!—
Since grief and joy must alike be ours,
  Why do we still complain?

Ever our failing, from sun to sun
  O my intolerant brother:—
We want just a little too little of one,
  And much too much of the other.

                    —James Whitcomb Riley

JANE WATSON HOPPING

Mysterious, Imperious, Delirious Month

In August the summer harvest begins in earnest, gardens are full of fresh produce, beans hang thick on the vine, cucumbers lie in disarray throughout the patch, and tender squashes with names like Hybrid Gold Rush, Black Magic, Gray Zucchini, Bennings Green Tint, and Golden Crookneck are in abundance. Most of the season's blackberries, raspberries, and blueberries are picked throughout this month.

By mid-August, Santa Rosa plums in orchards and their wild cousins along streams hang thick on the boughs. Later in the month, Blue Damsons perfume the air and compete with ripening peaches for use in cobblers and pies. Peaches always take the lead for making shortcakes.

And as if such bounty were not enough, the fields are filled with tall-growing hardy flowering plants: wild asters, goldenrod, cosmos, and ripening weeds, all adding subtle beauty to the dry landscape.

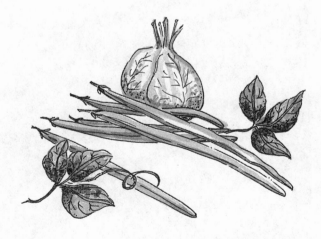

Oh! The Circus-Day Parade!

WHEN I WAS GROWING up, having a circus in town meant that everything else slowed down almost to a stop. People left their work to go out into the streets to see what all was goin' on. Farm families came into town on a weekday. Boys, twelve or even younger, played hooky from their chores and sneaked over to the fairgrounds to see if they could get a job setting up tents or doing anything else—just for the chance to be a part of all the excitement and glitter. Rumors flew as the town and country folk gossiped about jugglers, clowns, women in tights, lions, elephants, and monkeys. Posters went up and just before the show began, there was the eagerly awaited circus-day parade:

JANE WATSON HOPPING

THE CIRCUS-DAY PARADE

OH! the Circus-Day Parade! How the bugles played and played!
And the glossy horses tossed their flossy manes and neighed,
As the rattle and the rhyme of the tenor-drummer's time
Filled all the hungry hearts of us with melody sublime!

How the grand band-wagon shone with a splendor all its own,
And glittered with a glory that our dreams had never known!
And how the boys behind, high and low of every kind,
Marched in unconscious capture, with a rapture undefined!

How the horsemen, two and two, with their plumes of white and blue
And crimson, gold and purple, nodding by at me and you,
Waved the banners that they bore, as the knights in days of yore,
Till our glad eyes gleamed and glistened like the spangles that they wore!

How the graceless-graceful stride of the elephant was eyed,
And the capers of the little horse that cantered at his side!
How the shambling camels, tame to the plaudits of their fame,
With listless eyes came silent, masticating as they came.

How the cages jolted past, with each wagon battened fast,
And the mystery within it only hinted of at last
From the little grated square in the rear, and nosing there
The snout of some strange animal that sniffed the outer air!

And, last of all, The Clown, making mirth for all the town,
With his lips curved ever upward and his eyebrows ever down,
And his chief attention paid to the little mule that played
A tattoo on the dashboard with his heels, in the Parade.

Oh! the Circus-Day Parade! How the bugles played and played!
And how the glossy horses tossed their flossy manes and neighed,
As the rattle and the rhyme of the tenor-drummer's time
Filled all the hungry hearts of us with melody sublime!

—James Whitcomb Riley

CHICKEN IN RAMEKINS

makes 4 servings

THIS IS A FAVORITE leftover roast-chicken dish, perfect for bringing on a day-long outing. Auntie also thought it was a good way to stretch a chicken when you had many mouths to feed. Her recipe was a large one that made at least a dozen servings; ours is smaller.

3 tablespoons butter or margarine,
    plus 4 teaspoons for dotting
    individual portions
1 tablespoon all-purpose flour
1 teaspoon salt
¼ teaspoon black pepper

1 cup chicken broth (reserved from
    boiling leftover chicken carcass)
1 cup minced cooked chicken
1 cup cold boiled rice
4 tablespoons soft bread crumbs

Preheat oven to 350°F. Set out 4 lightly greased ramekins.

In a medium saucepan, melt *3 tablespoons butter,* add flour, salt, and pepper. Stir until well-blended. Add chicken broth and cook over medium heat until smooth and thickened. Add chicken and heat through. Spoon mixture equally into the ramekins.

Cover with rice and sprinkle with bread crumbs. Dot with *4 teaspoons butter.* Bake until contents are well heated and bread crumbs are browned, about 15 minutes.

JANE WATSON HOPPING

SUMMER-SQUASH MEDLEY

makes 6 to 8 servings

AT OUR HOUSE, IN season, summer squashes—zucchini, patty pan, and yellow crookneck—prepared in one way or another are daily fare. They are eaten boiled, steamed, fried, scalloped, and in this baked medley.

8 to 10 young summer squash, 4
    zucchini, 3 yellow crooknecks, 1
    patty pan
1 pound seasoned pork sausage
1 clove garlic, peeled and minced
½ large onion, peeled and diced
½ large green pepper, diced
4 large tomatoes, peeled and diced

1 teaspoon dried basil leaves,
    pulverized
1 teaspoon salt
¼ teaspoon black pepper
1½ cups bread crumbs
½ cup grated cheese (Swiss
    preferred)

Preheat oven to 350°F. Wash and slice squash; cover and set aside. Lightly grease a 13×9×2-inch baking dish.

In a large skillet, fry sausage until partially cooked—don't fry it hard and crumbly. Drain off excess fat. Add garlic and onion and fry 3 to 5 minutes more. Add green pepper, tomatoes, basil, salt, and pepper. Cover and let simmer for about 10 minutes, stirring occasionally.

Into the prepared baking dish, spread evenly *½ cup bread crumbs*. Spoon on one-third of hot tomato sauce and add half of mixed squash; add a second layer of bread crumbs and tomato sauce and top with remaining squash; end with remaining tomato sauce and top with the remaining *½ cup bread crumbs*.

Bake about 30 minutes, until squash is tender and pork done. Toward the last 15 minutes of cooking, sprinkle cheese over the top. Bake until cheese has melted and lightly browned. Remove from oven, serve immediately.

$\mathcal{A}$DA'S MACARONI SALAD

makes 4 to 6 servings

ABOUT 1931, ADA LEARNED to make this salad, and for a time she brought it to every picnic we had. Everyone loved it, and if she brought a different dish, various family members or friends came up and told her how much they enjoyed her macaroni salad and asked if she'd be bringing it to the next gathering.

1 pound fancy small macaroni
1 small jar pimientos, chopped fine, reserve 3 small pieces for garnish
1 medium sweet onion, chopped fine
3 small gherkins or sweet pickles, chopped fine

12 pitted ripe olives, reserve 4 for garnish
A drop or two of garlic juice
Mayonnaise

In a large saucepan of lightly salted water, cook macaroni, then drain. Pour into a large bowl. Add chopped pimientos, onion, pickles and stir; add olives and garlic juice, stirring to blend; moisten with mayonnaise. Turn into an attractive serving dish. Garnish with reserved pieces of pimiento and whole olives.

GERTRUDE'S FAVORITE BUTTER CAKE WITH PINEAPPLE FILLING AND PINEAPPLE BUTTER FROSTING

makes one 9-inch three-layer cake

GERTRUDE WAS A PERFECTIONIST, one who did everything just so. This lovely cake is an excellent example of the simple, old-fashioned butter cakes.

3 cups all-purpose flour
2½ teaspoons baking powder
½ teaspoon salt
¾ cup butter or margarine
1¾ cups sugar
4 eggs
1 cup cold water

1 teaspoon vanilla extract
½ teaspoon lemon extract
Pineapple Filling (recipe follows)
Pineapple Butter Frosting (recipe follows)

Preheat oven to 350°F. Lightly grease three round 9-inch layer-cake pans. Dust with flour and set aside.

Into a large bowl, sift flour, baking powder, and salt three times. In a second large bowl, cream butter and sugar until light. Break in 1 egg, 1 cup flour, and ⅓ cup water, and beat well; continue breaking in 1 egg and adding 1 cup flour and ⅓ cup water until flour and water are used up. Then add the final egg. Stir in vanilla and lemon extract. Pour batter into prepared cake pans. Bake until golden brown and firm to the touch, 35 to 40 minutes. Remove from oven; let set 10 minutes, then turn out onto wire racks to cool. When cool, fill and frost with Pineapple Filling and Pineapple Butter Frosting.

PINEAPPLE FILLING

makes enough to generously fill a two-layer cake or lightly fill a three-layer cake

2 tablespoons cornstarch
¼ cup sugar

2 cups crushed pineapple, drained
(reserve ¼ cup juice)

In a medium saucepan, blend cornstarch and sugar together. Add drained pineapple and cook until smooth and thickened. Blend in reserved *¼ cup juice*. Cool at room temperature.

PINEAPPLE BUTTER FROSTING

makes enough to frost a three-layer cake

3 cups powdered sugar
⅛ teaspoon salt
⅓ cup butter or margarine,
   softened at room temperature

½ cup well-drained crushed
   pineapple

In a medium bowl, blend sugar and salt into softened butter; beat until smooth. Add pineapple and mix well.

Foam Crested Waves, and Sandy Beach

FLORENCE MARY WARREN MCLEAN loved the outdoors, especially the beach, and was a deep mahogany tan all summer long. On Nantucket folks still recall her fast driving and cheerful whistling. "Tom," as everyone in her small town called her, after her father of chicken-raising and sulky-driving fame, never lingered in the past, always leaned into the future.

She was an extraordinary, instinctive cook, and even when dining alone prepared a decent meal. She could whip up a sweater, mittens, or doll clothes in no time. When she put the grandchildren to bed, she would tease them and say, "I love you a bushel and a peck and a hug around the neck!"

Independent and fun-loving, she was a self-made woman who worked hard as a housekeeper, housecleaner, or waitress to raise her children, Mary Lou and her sister Joan. And she adored and lavished attention on her ten grandchildren —three boys and seven girls.

Nowadays, when the family gathers, they speak with awe about the strength and spirit of their dear Nana, and the vitality of her life story. Her daughters credit her with the fact that they both have become happy, steady, well-adjusted women who love their own families. And they marvel how she managed to leave a wonderful legacy not only of memories, laughter and love, but of land, a precious bit of Nantucket for each of her grandchildren.

NANA'S BEACH

ALL I ask is a sunny day with
　　White clouds a flying,
Foam crested waves, and sandy beach,
　　And the sea gulls a crying.

All I ask is for sun-browned children,
　　The sound of merry laughter,
A quiet sleep and sweeter dreams,
　　Now and forever after.

—Jane Watson Hopping

JOHN RAE

JANE WATSON HOPPING

192

$\mathscr{N}$ANA'S CHOCOLATE POUND CAKE

makes 1 loaf

WHEN MEG'S AUNT JOAN was asked which recipe of Nana's should be included here, her immediate response was "Your grandmother made a mean pound cake!" And Meg agreed, remembering that this special cake arrived in tins throughout her freshman year of college, along with lots of letters and a hand-made afghan.

1 cup boiling water
2 squares (2 ounces) unsweetened
    baking chocolate
2 cups all-purpose flour
1 teaspoon baking soda
¼ teaspoon salt

½ cup butter or margarine
1¾ cups light brown sugar, firmly
    packed
2 eggs
1 teaspoon vanilla extract
½ cup dairy sour cream

Preheat oven to 325°F. Pour boiling water into a small bowl and melt chocolate in it; set aside to cool. Thoroughly grease a 9 × 5 × 3-inch loaf pan.

In a medium bowl, sift flour, soda, and salt. In a large bowl, cream butter, sugar, eggs, and vanilla until light and fluffy. Alternately, add flour mixture with the sour cream, blending well, then beat in the cooled chocolate-water mixture.

Bake until well risen, lightly browned, and firm to the touch, about 1 hour. Remove from oven and cool on the rack 15 minutes; then turn out onto the rack. Reverse the loaf so that it is top side up. Serve plain.

$\mathcal{L}$IL'S BLUEBERRY CAKE

makes 8 or more generous servings

SUMMER ON NANTUCKET MEANT beach days and blueberries. Assembling half a dozen kids for a swim can take time, so Nana would whip this cake up while waiting for the necessary pails, shovels, towels, snacks, and pals to be gathered. Then she would stuff the whole crowd into her old car and carry us to the small harborside sandspit her family still calls "Nana's Beach." Every so often Nana's daughters and grandchildren still sneak down to Nana's Beach for a late spring or early fall picnic. The path is bordered with tangles of sweet peas and daisies. It's a magical place, and they can almost hear their dear grandmother shouting out praise for their old underwater feats!

2 cups all-purpose flour	1 teaspoon salt
1½ cups sugar	2 eggs, separated
⅔ cup cold butter or margarine	1 cup milk
2 teaspoons baking powder	1 cup blueberries

Preheat oven to 350°F. Grease well and lightly flour a $13 \times 9 \times 2$-inch baking pan. Set aside until needed.

In a large bowl, sift flour and sugar together. Using a pastry blender or fingertips, cut in the butter until mixture looks like small peas. (Set aside *¾ cup* of this mixture for topping.) Add to *remaining flour* mixture the baking powder, salt, and combined egg yolks and milk. Beat until light (about 3 minutes at low speed if using an electric mixer). Using a rotary beater, whisk, or electric mixer, beat egg whites until stiff peaks form. Fold into the batter. Spread the batter into the prepared pan. Arrange berries over the batter and sprinkle with reserved *¾ cup crumb topping*.

Bake until batter is well risen, golden brown, and the berries are done (staining the cake in rich blueberry hues), about 45 to 50 minutes.

$\mathcal{N}$EW ENGLAND GOODIES

makes nearly 100 cookies

SPENDING A LITTLE TIME with her grandmother's old recipe book has been a heartwarming trip down memory lane for our friend Meg. Thoughtfully she tells us that not a day has passed since her dear grandmother died that she doesn't think of her in some way or another. These New England Goodies were a favorite treat for her flock of grandchildren.

4 cups all-purpose flour	1 cup sugar
2 teaspoons ground cinnamon	¾ cup butter or margarine,
1½ teaspoons salt	softened at room temperature
1 teaspoon instant coffee	2 eggs, well beaten
1 teaspoon ground ginger	1 cup light molasses
1 teaspoon baking soda	2 cups chocolate bits

Preheat oven to 350°F. Lightly grease one large or two smaller baking sheets. Set aside.

Into a large bowl, sift together, flour, cinnamon, salt, instant coffee, ginger and soda. In a second large bowl, cream sugar and butter together until light. Add eggs and molasses, beat thoroughly. Add flour mixture, alternately with milk. Stir in the chocolate bits. Drop by level tablespoons onto prepared baking sheet.

Bake until well risen, lightly browned and firm to the touch about 12 to 14 minutes. As each batch is done, remove from oven and transfer with a spatula to a brown paper or wire rack to cool. When thoroughly cooled, store in an airtight container.

God Bless the Patient Man

UNCLE BUD WAS A gentle man who loved his farm, his family, and all of us. He was the kind of man that folks just took to. All of the neighbors knew that if trouble came their way, they could call on Bud to come and give a hand, and that once he was there, things would usually work out all right. The Preacher called him a good Samaritan. And Alicia Hart told Auntie, "If you ever want to get rid of Bud, I'll be waiting at the front of the line to take him off your hands."

WHO BIDES HIS TIME

WHO bides his time, and day by day
    Faces defeat full patiently,
And lifts a mirthful roundelay,
    However poor his fortunes be,—
He will not fail in any qualm
    Of poverty—the paltry dime
It will grow golden in his palm,
      Who bides his time.

Who bides his time—he tastes the sweet
    Of honey in the saltest tear;
And though he fares with slowest feet,
    Joy runs to meet him, drawing near;
The birds are heralds of his cause;
    And, like a never-ending rhyme,
The roadsides bloom in his applause
      Who bides his time.

Who bides his time, and fevers not
    In the hot race that none achieves,
Shall wear cool-wreathen laurel, wrought
    With crimson berries in the leaves;
And he shall reign a goodly king,
    And sway his hand o'er every clime
With peace writ on his signet-ring,
      Who bides his time.

—James Whitcomb Riley

JANE WATSON HOPPING

196

RASPBERRY CROWDIE CREAM

makes about 4 servings

THIS TRADITIONAL SCOTTISH DESSERT is a mixture of whipped cream and toasted oats. Granny, who farmed alone, had a good Jersey cow and a long row of Cumberland raspberries, which she served with the crowdie cream. The Cumberland raspberry, like all black-cap varieties, is a hardy mid-season berry, one that is glossy-black and firm. The berries are easily picked, and when handled hold their shape without crumbling, which makes them not only fine for eating fresh, but excellent for canning and for making jellies and jams.

⅓ cup dry quick or old-fashioned oats
1 cup cold heavy cream
¼ cup powdered sugar

2 tablespoons brandy
1½ cups Cumberland raspberries (red varieties may be substituted)

Preheat oven to 350°F. Thinly scatter oats over a shallow ungreased baking pan. Bake until toasted, about 6 to 8 minutes (oats should be tan-colored and crisp). Remove toasted oats from the oven and set aside to cool.

In a medium bowl, whip cream until it begins to thicken, then gradually add powdered sugar, *1 tablespoon* at a time. Continue whipping cream until stiff peaks form (don't overbeat or cream will taste greasy). Gently stir in brandy *1 teaspoon* at a time. Fold in toasted oats. Top with unsweetened raspberries and serve immediately.

AMETHYST RASPBERRY TARTS WITH COOKIE CRUST TART SHELLS

makes 8 servings

GRANDPA LIKED SODUS AND Amethyst raspberries. These purple berries are a cross between the red and black varieties. Both are large, firm, and sweet tasting. They grow well in most soils, are resistant to temperature changes, and are firm enough to can well. Grandpa's Amethysts were excellent producers, yielding 5½ to 6 pints per bush.

Cookie Crust Tart Shells (recipe
    follows)
1 quart ripe raspberries, freshly
    picked
¼ cup cold water, plus
    3 tablespoons for
    moistening cornstarch

3 tablespoons sugar
1½ tablespoons cornstarch
Sweetened Whipped Cream
    (page 17)

Make and bake tart shells.

Put raspberries in a sieve and gently run cold tap water through them; drain. Into a small bowl, puree *1 cup raspberries* by pressing them through a small sieve or colander. Add *¼ cup cold water* and sugar. With a spatula, scrape puree into a small saucepan and bring to a boil. Add cornstarch, moistened with *3 tablespoons cold water,* all at once, stirring constantly until filling is clear, 3 to 5 minutes. Set aside to cool.

Just before serving, fill baked tart shells with remaining *3 cups raspberries* (unsweetened or lightly sweetened, as you wish). Pour cooled filling over the fresh raspberries and refrigerate 30 minutes. Serve each with a generous dollop of Sweetened Whipped Cream.

*C*OOKIE CRUST TART SHELLS

makes six 3-inch tart shells

1 cup sifted all-purpose flour
2 tablespoons sugar
¼ teaspoon salt

⅓ cup cold butter or margarine
1 egg yolk, well beaten
1½ tablespoons cold water

Preheat oven to 450°F. Set out 6 tart-shell pans.

In a medium bowl, stir together flour, sugar, and salt. Using a pastry blender or the fingertips, work in butter until mixture resembles coarse cornmeal. Then, stir in the egg yolk and *1 tablespoon cold water*. Add remaining ½ *tablespoon* if needed to make a soft pliable dough that will not stick to the hands. Turn dough out onto a lightly floured surface. Roll to ⅛-inch thickness. Line the tart pans with the dough. Trim edges and place dry beans in each cup to weight down pastry.

Bake in 400°F oven until shells are lightly browned, 8 to 10 minutes. When done, unmold pastry shells and cool on a wire rack.

RED-RASPBERRY VINEGAR

makes two 1-pint bottles of raspberry vinegar

OLD-TIME WOMEN USED TO make any number of kinds of vinegar. They kept a vinegar crock in the pantry, covered with a clean dish towel, and added the sweetened juices that were poured off opened home-canned fruit. They also rinsed the sugar bowl before washing it and added the sweetened water to the contents of the vinegar crock, thus making household vinegars of varying strengths and flavors. Besides such utilitarian vinegar, they made brown sugar, honey, and fruit vinegars for their special tonics and for cooking purposes.

2 dried red hibiscus flowers
   (see note)
1 pint red raspberries

1 quart white vinegar (light-colored wine vinegar that will not overpower the raspberry flavor may be substituted)

Wash and thoroughly sterilize two 1-pint wine bottles with corks (sterilize the corks too). Push 1 hibiscus flower through the neck of each bottle and shake it down to the bottom. Gently rinse raspberries under a small stream of cold tap water (too much rinsing will dilute the flavor). Drip-dry and divide berries, dropping one by one into each bottle.

Pour vinegar into each bottle, leaving only enough room to cork. Put the cork firmly in place and set the bottles of flavored vinegar in a cool, dark, dry place to blend. Over a two-week period, swirl the contents of the bottles occasionally to distribute the flavors (don't shake).

When the raspberry flavor can be tasted in the vinegar, it is ready for use in salads.

NOTE: Dried red hibiscus flowers may be purchased in food specialty shops. They naturally give the vinegar a lovely pink color and a distinct fruity flavor.

Mellow Hazes, Lowly Trailing Over Wood and Meadow

A DREAM OF AUTUMN

MELLOW hazes, lowly trailing
  Over wood and meadow, veiling
Somber skies, with wild fowl sailing
  Sailor-like to foreign lands;
And the north wind overleaping
Summer's brink, and flood-like sweeping
Wrecks of roses where the weeping-
  Willows wring their helpless hands.

—James Whitcomb Riley

SEPTEMBER, WITH ITS HOT days and cool nights, is a glorious blend of summer and autumn; clear, bright mornings fade until in the late afternoon a golden haze touches the landscape, changing the commonplace into a thing of beauty.

AT AUNTY'S HOUSE

ONE time, when we'z at Aunty's house—
  'Way in the country!—where
They's ist but woods—an' pigs, an' cows—
  An' all's outdoors an' air!—
An' orchurd-swing; an' churry trees—
An' *churries* in 'em!—Yes, an' these-
Here redhead birds steals all they please,
  An' tetch 'em ef you dare!—
W'y, wunst, one time, when we wuz there,
  We et out on the porch!

Wite where the cellar door wuz shut
  The table wuz; an' I
Let Aunty set by me an' cut
  My vittuls up—an' pie.
'Tuz awful funny!—I could see
The redheads in the churry tree;
An' beehives, where you got to be
  So keerful, goin' by;—
An' "Comp'ny" there an' all!—an' we—
  We et out on the porch!

An' I ist et *p'surves* an' things
  'At Ma don't 'low me to—
An' *chickun-gizzurds*—(don't like *wings*
  Like *Parunts* does! do *you?*)
An' all the time the wind blowed there,
An' I could feel it in my hair,
An' ist smell clover *ever*'where!—
  An' a old redhead flew
Purt' nigh wite over my high-chair
  When we et on the porch!

—James Whitcomb Riley

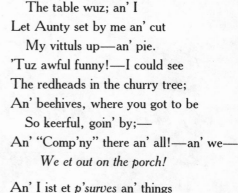

JANE WATSON HOPPING

The Sum of Their Laughter

IN SUMMER, NEIGHBORHOOD CHILDREN used to play with our children Randy and Colleen here on the farm. The girls loved to feed the chickens, cuddle the lambs, run through the field, and pick wild flowers. The boys, kicking and throwing balls this way and that, sometimes barely missed the windows. During those years, I grew boys and girls and a subsistence garden. There was little room or time in my life for playing with my flowers or reading books.

In those days, I could see from my kitchen windows Colleen and Traci, who were both quite small, clinging to the lower limbs of an ancient walnut tree, meowing and hissing, pretending to be kitty cats. And I could see the boys—Randy, Kenny, David, Tim, and others, a wild and boistrous band of healthy youngsters, tanned by the summer sun and made strong by vigorous activity; sometimes I thought they never rested.

About noon, a string of barefoot, bareheaded beggars would come to my back door, led by our son Randy, all of whom wondered if I had ice-cold milk and enough peanut butter and wild blackberry jelly for sandwiches. Often Colleen and Traci would already be on their knees in front of the open refrigerator, tipping an icy glass bottle of real farm milk into tall glasses, or searching cupboards for a gallon jar of freshly baked cookies.

When the afternoon heat drove the girls out of the fields and trees, they settled down in the shade with pet cats, ducks, and Terry, our little dog. The boys gathered, long legs a tangle under the kitchen table, to play cards or Monopoly. The games were always punctuated by riotous laughter, friendly argument, and a little arm punching.

Those glorious summers—when we all were young, vital, and living life to the hilt—were filled with joy. So often, I think of those days, and the pleasure and memories that lie nestled in my mind, and I can't help but think: *God bless the little ones, mine and all others!*

THE COUNTRY MOTHERS COOKBOOK

$\mathcal{H}$AM LOAF IN A BLANKET WITH MUSHROOM SAUCE

makes 8 servings

WHEN OUR CHILDREN WERE small, I worked very hard on the farm. It was my job to dispatch the haying crew, drive the truck when we hauled hay into the barn, raise a big garden, and put up our food for winter, take care of the children, help with the butchering, and sew, clean, and cook.

When the work load was heavy and the hours stretched out, supper became a pick-up meal of fresh sliced tomatoes, cucumbers, melons, bread and butter, and something warmed-over from the day before—or sometimes even a hamburger uptown. On Sundays I tried to cook a few things that would lighten my cooking load during the following week.

Crispy Biscuit Dough (recipe
    follows)
1 onion, chopped
3 tablespoons bacon drippings,
    butter, or margarine
2 cups finely chopped cooked
    potatoes

1½ cups chopped cooked ham
2 eggs
½ cup milk
½ teaspoon salt
½ teaspoon black pepper
Mushroom Sauce (recipe follows)

Before making the filling, prepare biscuit dough; cover and set aside. Preheat oven to 425°F. Set out a large baking sheet.

In a large skillet over medium heat, brown onion in fat. Add potatoes and mix well. Stir in ham, eggs, milk, salt, and pepper. Heat thoroughly. Roll out biscuit dough into rectangle ¼ inch thick. Shape hot ham mixture into a loaf centered on the dough. Draw dough up over mixture to form a roll, pressing edges of dough firmly together. Slash top, place loaf on baking sheet, and bake 15 to 20 minutes. Serve sliced, with Mushroom Sauce.

CRISPY BISCUIT DOUGH

2 cups sifted all-purpose flour
½ teaspoon baking soda
½ teaspoon salt

4 tablespoons cold butter or
    margarine
About ¾ cup buttermilk

Into a large bowl, sift flour, soda, and salt. Using a pastry blender (or finger-tips), work fat into flour until mixture resembles coarse cornmeal. Add butter-milk to make a soft dough (this may take 1 tablespoon more or less milk, depending on the dryness of the flour).

Turn onto lightly floured surface. Knead 4 or 5 times to form a smooth ball. Cover while making filling.

MUSHROOM SAUCE

makes 2 cups

3 cups button mushrooms
3 tablespoons butter
3 tablespoons all-purpose flour
1½ cups stock or milk

½ teaspoon salt
⅛ teaspoon black pepper
2 tablespoons minced pimientos,
    more if you wish

Sauté mushrooms in butter 5 minutes, then blend in flour. Add stock and cook until thickened, stirring constantly. Season and add pimientos.

$\mathcal{F}$RESH VEGETABLE SALADS AND MELONS

IN THE MIDWEST AND among transplanted midwestern families, green salads were rarely served. Old-time people more often used hot bacon fat, vinegar and a little water to wilt salad greens like spinach, swiss chard, beet tops, and various types of lettuce, often mixed with wild greens. Vegetables right out of the garden, like Ace or Beefsteak tomatoes, Straight Eight cucumbers, sweet half- or full-grown Sweet Spanish or Bermuda onions, bell peppers, and carrots, were peeled and sliced or just sliced, depending on the custom of the family, and set on the table in separate bowls or on plates and platters, to be eaten plain or with a little salt on them.

In addition to the vegetables, there were platters of melons: banana, honey-dew, muskmelons (cantaloupes) of every ilk, sometimes even watermelon, all gathered before the meal, or taken out of a cool storage for it.

$\mathcal{P}$EACH MELBA

makes 6 portions

AUNT ALICE, WHO WITH her brothers immigrated from England shortly after the turn of the century, once told Mother that this lovely dessert was created in the late 1800s by the famed French chef Escoffier, and that he named it Peach Melba in honor of the Australian operatic soprano Nellie Melba.

1 cup sugar, plus ¼ cup for
    raspberry topping
1 cup water
1 teaspoon vanilla extract

3 large (about 1 pound) firm ripe
    peaches
2 cups (1 pint) ripe red raspberries
1 quart vanilla ice cream

In a saucepan, combine *1 cup sugar* and water. Place over medium heat and bring to a boil, stirring constantly. Cover and boil 5 minutes. Remove from heat and add vanilla.

Rinse, peel, cut into halves, and pit peaches (quickly blot off excess juice with paper towel). Over medium heat, add peach halves to syrup, two at a time, and simmer about 3 minutes. Using a slotted spoon, carefully remove cooked peaches from syrup, letting the excess syrup drip into the saucepan. Repeat with remaining peach halves. Chill peaches in refrigerator.

Meanwhile, rinse raspberries gently by allowing a little cold tap water to run through them; don't stir. Drain and force through a coarse sieve or food mill. Stir in remaining ¼ *cup sugar*. Chill.

To serve, spoon ice cream into a large glass dish; arrange peaches over ice cream cut sides down, and top with raspberry sauce. Serve immediately.

*B*ILLY GOAT GRUFF COOKIES

makes 3 to 3½ dozen cookies

ONCE UPON A TIME, three billy goats lived in a stony field near a bridge that stretched across a little river. They were Great Big Billy Goat Gruff, Big Billy Goat Gruff, and Little Billy Goat Gruff . . .

3 cups sifted all-purpose flour
¼ teaspoon freshly grated nutmeg
1 cup cold butter or margarine
1½ cups firmly packed light brown
    sugar

½ teaspoon vanilla extract
3 eggs, well beaten
About ½ cup powdered sugar

Preheat oven to 425°F. Set out a large baking sheet.

Into a large bowl, sift flour with nutmeg. Using a pastry blender, cut butter into flour mixture until mixture has the texture of coarse cornmeal. Add sugar and blend with flour mixture. Combine vanilla and eggs and stir into dry ingredients, blending to form a ball of dough. Turn out on lightly floured surface and roll ⅛ inch thick. Sprinkle with powdered sugar, then cut with a doughnut cutter. Lay cookies on baking sheet.

Bake until light tan around the edges, 10 to 12 minutes. Watch baking time carefully as these cookies are topped with sugar and burn easily in the hot oven. As each batch is done, remove from oven. Transfer immediately to brown paper or wire racks to cool. When thoroughly cooled, store in an airtight container.

Old John

IN OUR AREA, THERE lived an old man, a bachelor who didn't seem to have any family. Mother would take us children and go over to see him with a plate of cookies or loaf of fresh bread. They would visit, and he would show us all of his flowers and send us home with a large bouquet:

> HE knew the flowers by name, and though a man was he,
> Blood-brother to the daffodil and rose he seemed to be.
> He'd lived his life among them, and when spring is in the air,
> There'll be sorrow in the garden for Old John will not be there.
>
> From dawn to dusk he labored through the years among the flowers,
> And I'm sure he lived a richer and a happier life than ours,
> For his face was calm and placid, and he never seemed to care
> For the glory that is business or the crown that skill might wear.
>
> All his waking time was given to forget-me-nots and phlox,
> To his peonies and pansies, and his sturdy holly-hocks;
> And I've watched him many a summer bending over bloomy beds,
> Just as tender as a mother stroking little curly heads.
>
> Now the Lord has called him yonder, and the spring is coming on,
> And the tulips and the jonquils will be asking: "Where is John?"
> And I'm wondering what the roses and forget-me-nots will say
> When the word is passed among them that "Old John" has gone away.

—Edgar A. Guest

JANE WATSON HOPPING

208

THE COUNTRY MOTHERS COOKBOOK

209

GRANDMA HOSKIN'S RED-ROSE HONEY

makes about 3 half-pints

WOMEN OF THE PAST often used rose petals for flavoring. In this recipe, they add color as well as flavor.

3 fragrant red roses
3 cups honey (light-colored
   preferred)
1 cup water

About ⅛ teaspoon rock alum (sold
   with pickle-making supplies in
   grocery stores)

Pick roses early in the morning while the dew is still on them. Rinse very lightly in running cold water. Remove petals, discarding all else. In a medium saucepan, combine petals, honey, and water; bring to a gradual boil over medium heat. Add rock alum. Continue boiling until syrup is thick. Strain through cheesecloth while still hot. Pour into scrubbed and sterilized half-pint jars. Seal with hot sterilized lids and rings. (Lid is sealed when it is concave.) Store in a cool dry place.

THE YELLOWBIRD

HEY! my little Yellowbird,
   What are you doing there?
Like a flashing sun-ray,
   Flitting everywhere:
Dangling down the tall weeds
   And the hollyhocks,
And the lordly sunflowers
   Along the garden-walks.

Ho! my gallant Golden-bill,
   Pecking 'mongst the weeds,
You must have for breakfast
   Golden flower-seeds:
Won't you tell a little fellow
   What you have for *tea?*—
'Spect a peck o' yellow, mellow
   Pippin on the tree.

—James Whitcomb Riley

JANE WATSON HOPPING

OLD-FASHIONED COFFEE CAKES

makes about 2 dozen cakes

THIS FAMILY-SIZE RECIPE, WHICH dates back over a hundred years, is plain but good when eaten hot at breakfast, teatime, or just before going to bed. We would probably call them cookies.

1 cup butter or margarine, softened at room temperature
2 cups firmly packed light brown sugar
1 cup milk
3 eggs, well beaten
4 cups sifted all-purpose flour

1 teaspoon baking soda
2 teaspoons cream of tartar
About 2 teaspoons ground cinnamon, more if desired
About 1 cup granulated sugar for dipping cakes

Preheat oven to 375°F. Grease a large baking sheet; set aside.

In a large bowl, cream butter and brown sugar until well blended. Add milk and eggs, stirring well. Sift flour with soda and cream of tartar. Add flour mixture to liquid ingredients. Stir into a stiff dough. Turn onto a lightly floured surface and knead 3 or 4 times or until dough forms a cohesive ball that does not stick to the hands. Then roll out to ½-inch thickness. Sprinkle cinnamon over dough and roll up like a jelly roll. Pinch rolled edge to hold dough together. Slice into ½-inch-thick slices. Drop one at a time into granulated sugar, coating only one side.

Bake sugared side up until light golden brown, about 20 to 25 minutes. Remove from oven and let set about 5 minutes, then serve out of the pan while still hot.

MRS. HOVIN'S WHITE CAKE WITH SEVEN-MINUTE FROSTING

makes one 9-inch two-layer cake

GRANDPA WAS BORN IN 1875, and all during his childhood this was a popular go-to-meetin' cake served with tea or coffee while folks visited before starting the long drive home over rough country roads; it was still popular when Mother was a little girl; and today, when made into a two-layer cake and frosted with Seven-Minute Frosting, it wins praise. This cake and frosting use egg whites only. On farms, the unused yolks were often cooked and given to dogs, cats, chickens, or piglets.

1 cup butter, softened at room temperature	⅓ cup cornstarch
1 cup sugar	2 teaspoons baking powder
½ cup milk	½ teaspoon salt
1½ cups all-purpose flour	Whites of 5 eggs
	Seven-Minute Frosting (page 213)

Preheat oven to 350°F. Lightly grease and flour two round 9-inch layer-cake pans.

In a large bowl, cream butter and sugar together until light. Add milk and stir until well blended. Into a medium bowl, sift flour with cornstarch, baking powder, and salt. Add flour mixture to butter-sugar mixture, stirring until well blended. Beat egg whites until soft peaks form and fold in carefully so as not to stir down volume. Turn into prepared cake pans.

Bake until well risen and light golden brown on top, 30 to 35 minutes. Test by sticking a toothpick into the center of one of the layers. If it comes out clean, both are done. Remove from oven, cool about 10 minutes, then turn out of pans onto wire racks. Cool thoroughly before frosting with Seven-Minute Frosting.

SEVEN-MINUTE FROSTING

fills and frosts one 9-inch two-layer cake

2 egg whites
1½ cups sugar
⅓ cup water

Dash of salt (less than ⅛ teaspoon)
1 teaspoon light corn syrup
1 teaspoon vanilla extract

Fill the base of a double boiler about ⅓ full of water, cover with lid and bring to a boil. In the top pan, combine egg whites, sugar, the *⅓ cup water,* salt, and corn syrup. Beat with rotary beater until well blended. Then, place top pan over bottom (which should now be boiling rapidly).

Beat contents of top pan constantly at high speed; continue cooking and beating until frosting hangs in stiff peaks on the beater when it is removed, about 7 minutes. Scrape sides and bottom of cooking pan frequently while the frosting cooks.

When frosting is stiff, remove top pan from double boiler. Add vanilla and beat until frosting is thick enough to spread, about 1 to 2 minutes. (At this point the pan should not be scraped too closely, as it may cause the frosting to crystallize.

There's Somethin'
About October

IN OCTOBER, SHRIVELED WILD grapes, tenuously hanging in trees along the creek, leaves rattling and tan, yielding to the season's chill, appear to be a prophetic sign of winter drawing nigh. And then incongruously come the warm, hazy days of Indian summer, with their piquant autumn tang. Everywhere, leaves turn brilliant crimson, russet, and gold. Wild asters, fringed gentian, and goldenrod enrich the natural beauty of the countryside. Summer insects are killed in the first frost, songbirds flee south, country people are hard about the harvest.

There's somethin' about October that dredges up fond recollections of the springtime of our lives. The early frost urges us to live life heartily while the warmth lasts. Hazy later days passionately call out to us:

LOVELY, LOVELY OCTOBER

ERE, in the northern gale,
The summer tresses of the trees are gone,
The woods of Autumn, all around our vale,
Have put their glory on.

—William Cullen Bryant

JANE WATSON HOPPING

A-Livin' All Alone There in That Lonesome Sort o' Way

IN THE OLD DAYS, survival depended on cooperative work, roles played were like a dance in which the movement of each enriched that of the other. Death came easy through childbirth, old age, accident, and natural disasters, and brought with it a tragic blow that wreaked not only great sorrow but economic hardships on the surviving family.

How It Happened

I GOT to thinkin' of her—both her parents dead and gone—
And all her sisters married off, and none but her and John
A-livin' all alone there in that lonesome sort o' way,
And him a blame old bachelor, confirmder ev'ry day!
I'd knowed 'em all from children, and their daddy from the time
He settled in the neighberhood, and hadn't ary a dime
Er dollar, when he married, fer to start housekeepin' on!—
So I got to thinkin' of her—both her parents dead and gone!

I got to thinkin' of her; and a-wundern what she done
That all her sisters kep' a gittin' married, one by one,
And her without no chances—and the best girl of the pack—
An old maid, with her hands, you might say, tied behind her back!
And Mother, too, afore she died, she ust to jes' take on,
When none of 'em was left, you know, but Evaline and John,
And jes' declare to goodness 'at the young men must be bline
To not see what a wife they'd git if they got Evaline!

I got to thinkin' of her; in my great affliction she
Was sich a comfort to us, and so kind and neighberly,—
She'd come, and leave her housework, fer to he'p out little Jane,
And talk of *her own* mother 'at she'd never see again—
Maybe sometimes cry together—though, fer the most part she
Would have the child so riconciled and happy-like 'at we
Felt lonesomer 'n ever when she'd put her bonnet on
And say she'd railly haf to be a-gittin' back to John!

I got to thinkin' of her, as I say,—and more and more
I'd think of her dependence, and the burdens 'at she bore,—
Her parents both a bein' dead, and all her sisters gone
And married off, and her a-livin' there alone with John—
You might say jes' a-toilin' and a-slavin' out her life
Fer a man 'at hadn't pride enough to git hisse'f a wife—
'Less some one married *Evaline* and packed her off some day!—
So I got to thinkin' of her—and it happened thataway.

—James Whitcomb Riley

JANE WATSON HOPPING

216

$\mathcal{V}$ENISON POT ROAST WITH VEGETABLES

makes 6 to 8 servings

IN THE 1800s MANY people still cooked in great iron pots that hung on cranes over the fire, or in Dutch ovens buried among the coals.

One 3- to 4-pound venison roast
    (cuts from chuck, round, or
    rump preferred)
¼ cup cubed salt pork or mild
    bacon
2 tablespoons butter or margarine
1½ cups hot water
1 cup apple cider
1 stalk celery, sliced
1 tablespoon chopped fresh parsley

¼ teaspoon dried thyme,
    pulverized
1 teaspoon salt plus about
    ½ teaspoon more for salting
    vegetables
¼ teaspoon black pepper
6 whole carrots, peeled
6 whole small onions, peeled
6 whole medium potatoes, peeled

Make several small slits in the roast, then lard by inserting cubes of salt pork into the cuts. Meanwhile heat butter in a Dutch oven, taking care not to burn the butter. Put larded meat into the Dutch oven and brown on all sides. Add hot water, cider, celery, parsley, thyme, salt, and pepper. Cover and simmer gently over medium-low heat until meat is tender, about 3 hours. Check frequently. If the liquid gets too low, add more water.

About 1 hour before the meal is to be served (after the meat has been cooking for about 2 hours), add the carrots, onions, and potatoes. Salt vegetables lightly. When vegetables are tender, transfer the meat to a large platter; surround it with the vegetables (or put them in a separate serving dish). Cover and keep hot while making gravy (see page 218).

GRAVY

makes about 4 cups

4 cups pot liquor
6 tablespoons butter or margarine

6 tablespoons all-purpose flour
Salt and pepper to taste

Measure the pot liquor and add enough water (if needed) to make 4 cups. In the empty Dutch oven, put the butter and melt over medium-high heat. When melted, stir in flour. Let flour cook until it browns a little, then pour pan liquor back into the Dutch oven and stir constantly to blend. Continue stirring until the gravy thickens and becomes somewhat clear (not as clear as when made with cornstarch).

BAKED ACORN SQUASH TOPPED WITH TOASTED PEANUTS

makes 6 servings

UNCLE BUD BUILT SHELVES on his back porch near the hot-water tank for storing his winter squashes, among them a dozen or so acorn squash. Before he and Auntie had a hot-water heater on the porch, they used to store the squashes in the kitchen, close to the stove.

3 medium acorn squash, washed,
    cut into halves crosswise, seeds
    and fibers removed
Boiling water
½ cup butter or margarine, melted

1½ tablespoons light brown sugar
½ teaspoon salt
¼ teaspoon ground ginger
⅛ teaspoon ground nutmeg
½ cup toasted peanuts

Preheat oven to 400°F. Set out a large shallow baking pan.

Put the prepared squash halves cut side down in the baking dish. Pour boiling water into the dish to ½-inch level. Bake squash until partially cooked,

JANE WATSON HOPPING

about 30 minutes. Remove from oven and turn cavity side up. Fill the centers with equal amounts of melted butter and a mixture of brown sugar, salt, ginger, and nutmeg.

Return squash to oven and bake until tender when pierced with a fork, about 25 minutes longer. Top with toasted peanuts. Serve piping hot.

$\mathcal{M}$OCK OYSTERS

makes 6 to 8 servings

OLD-TIME PEOPLE CALLED SALSIFY—an ancient vegetable—the oyster plant or vegetable oyster because the flavor of its long white root reminded them of the taste of oysters. Grandpa always said that salsify is hard to raise because it is slow growing and exacting in its need for acid, fertilizer, and weather conditions.

Nevertheless, farm folks that loved the vegetable oyster didn't let its persnickety ways slow them down, and would work willingly and long to raise oyster plants even though the yield was often disappointing.

1 to 2 pounds salsify
Few drops lemon juice or vinegar
2 tablespoons butter, plus butter for
    cooking
1 tablespoon thick cream
¼ teaspoon salt

¼ teaspoon black pepper
1 teaspoon lemon juice or cider
    vinegar
1 egg, beaten
Bread crumbs

Wash and scrape each root, dropping it into a saucepan of cold water to which a few drops of lemon juice or vinegar have been added. Add water to stand halfway up the salsify. Simmer until tender. When done, drain and rub through a colander. Mix into a smooth puree with *2 tablespoons butter,* cream, salt, pepper, and lemon juice or cider vinegar. Let the puree chill. When chilled, form into small flat cakes about the size of an oyster. Dip cakes into beaten egg and finely rolled bread crumbs. Fry lightly in butter until golden brown and crisp.

Gentle Memories of Home

HOMESTEADS ON THE CUTTING edge of civilization were rustic, simple, often hardscrabble farms, but old-time memories of them speak gently and lovingly of tight-knit families, the beauty of the natural surroundings, and the joy of self-reliance:

JANE WATSON HOPPING

From A CHILD'S HOME—LONG AGO

EVEN as the gas-flames flicker to and fro,
The Old Man's wavering fancies leap and glow,—
As o're the vision, like a mirage, falls
The old log cabin with its dingy walls,
And crippled chimney with its crutch-like prop
Beneath a sagging shoulder at the top;
The coon-skin battened fast on either side—
The wisps of leaf-tobacco—"cut-and-dried";
The yellow strands of quartered apples, hung
In rich festoons that tangle in among
The morning-glory vines that clamber o'er
The little clap-board roof above the door:
The old well-sweep that drops a courtesy
To every thirsting soul so graciously,
The stranger, as he drains the dipping gourd,
Intuitively murmurs, "Thank the Lord!"
Again through mists of memory arise
The simple scenes of home before the eyes:
The happy mother, humming, with her wheel,
The dear old melodies that used to steal
So drowsily upon the summer air,
The house-dog hid his bone, forgot his care,
And nestled at her feet, to dream, perchance,
Some cooling dream of wintertime romance.

—James Whitcomb Riley

The Farm Security Loan

IN ORDER TO GET the nation's raw materials flowing again, the federal government in 1939 decided to loan farmers money. Herman and Vera, friends from Kansas, were struggling along on about six hundred dollars a year when they heard about the Farm Security Loan. So, needing a team of workhorses, a couple of brood sows, a milk cow, some equipment and supplies, they applied.

Among the requirements they had to meet in order to qualify was the submission of a very detailed budget. Herman doesn't quite laugh when he tells about that budget and the loan officer's insistence that they include ten dollars a year for recreation. Seeing in that ten dollars another hog or several bags of feed or seed, Herman told him that they didn't need to borrow money for recreation. (Needless to say, the ten dollars went into the budget.)

Another requirement was that they be self-sufficient: that they raise and process their own food. To ensure compliance, the government insisted that

JANE WATSON HOPPING

they include a pressure cooker in their budget. Since practically no one in southeastern Kansas had ever seen, much less used, such a newfangled gadget, the cost seemed wasteful to the Kampings. Besides, they had all kinds of survival skills.

As it was, they had a garden, chickens, a few animals, and a good rifle and shotgun for hunting. They knew how to dry fruit and vegetables; pack sauerkraut and pickles down in barrels; layer a few beans, corn, and herbs down between layers of salt in a crock. They put up fruit in whatever tin cans they could afford and cured meat in salt brine.

Even so, they soon learned that if you wanted the government loan, you bought a pressure cooker. And when it came, the whole Kamping family turned out to see it work. It was a tall, heavy kettle that held seven half-gallon jars (women canned in large jars for large families) or two layers of smaller ones. All around the lid were thumbscrews that when tightened down kept the pressure from blowing the lid off and doing unimaginable things to the contents.

After much confusion, they all decided to put prepared meat, as they had always fixed it for canning, in the cooker to test it out. The lid was put on and screwed down, the pressure was up, the time carefully watched, the pressure exhausted, a cooling time allowed, and finally the lid unscrewed and removed.

Herman and Vera both laugh as he tells about the "real stew" they had inside—meat, metal cans, lard, and beeswax—all floating around together.

From FARMYARD SONG

INTO the yard the farmer goes,
With grateful heart, at the close of day;
Harness and chain are hung away;
In the wagon shed stand yoke and plow;
The straw's in the stack, the hay in the mow,
    The cooling dews are falling;—
The friendly sheep his welcome bleat,
The pigs come grunting to his feet,
The whinnying mare her master knows,
When into the yard the farmer goes,
    His cattle calling,—
"Co', boss! co', boss! co! co! co!"

—J. T. Trowbridge

THE COUNTRY MOTHERS COOKBOOK

VERA'S APPLE DUMPLINGS

makes 6 dumplings

VERA KAMPING, FARMER'S WIFE and long-time Grange member, bakes some of the best pies I've ever tasted. Many thanks to her for teaching me to make Apple Dumplings.

Double-Crust Pastry (page 156)
6 baking apples, peeled and cored
   (Rome Beauty or Cortland
   preferred)
3 tablespoons butter, melted

Ground cinnamon as desired (less
   than ⅛ teaspoon per apple)
Sugar to taste (about 1½ teaspoons
   per apple)
Syrup (recipe follows)

Make pastry and chill. Then just before assembling dumplings, turn onto a lightly floured surface and roll out. Cut into 6 squares large enough to make an envelope or case for each apple. Preheat oven to 375°F. Set out a 12 × 9 × 2-inch baking dish.

    Working with one apple at a time, fill with butter, sugar, and cinnamon and set in the center of a pastry square; fold the pastry up around the apple and press the seams together to make a dumpling. Arrange dumplings in the baking dish, leaving space between apples. Prepare syrup and pour it boiling hot over the dumplings.

    Bake, basting frequently, until syrup is absorbed and dumplings have browned, about 1 hour. Remove from oven. Set on a wire rack to cool. Serve warm or cold with or without cream on top.

SYRUP

¾ cup sugar
1 cup water

2 tablespoons butter

In a saucepan, heat sugar, water, and butter until sugar is dissolved and butter melted. Bring to a boil. Remove from heat and pour over dumplings.

JANE WATSON HOPPING

A NONSENSE CALENDAR

YOU wouldn't believe
On All Hallow Eve
What lots of fun we can make,
With apples to bob,
And nuts on the hob,
And a ring-and-thimble cake.

A paper boat
We will set afloat,
And on it write a name;
Then salt we'll burn
And our fortunes learn
From a flickering candle flame.

Tom said, "When it's dark
We can strike a spark
From the fur of the big black cat."
But I said, "No!
'T would tease kitty so—
And I love her too much for that."

—Carolyn Wells

The Gobble-uns'll Git You Ef You Don't Watch Out!

WHEN I WAS LITTLE, Halloween was a party at home with all the relatives. We would have a great potluck supper that featured all of the foods of summer, we played games like bob-for-apples, told ghost stories, and recited poetry about goblins:

LITTLE ORPHAN ANNIE

WUNST they wuz a little boy wouldn't say his prayers,—
An' when he went to bed at night, away up-stairs,
His Mammy heerd him holler, an' his Daddy heerd him bawl,
An' when they turn't the kivvers down, he wuzn't there at all!
An' they seeked him in the rafter-room, an' cubby-hole, an' press,
An' seeked him up the chimbly-flue, an' ever'wheres, I guess;
But all they ever found wuz thist his pants an' roundabout:—
An' the Gobble-uns 'll git you
         Ef you
            Don't
               Watch
                  Out!

An' one time a little girl 'ud allus laugh an' grin,
An' make fun of ever'one, an' all her blood-an'-kin;
An' wunst, when they was "company," an' ole folks wuz there,
She mocked 'em an' shocked 'em, an' said she didn't care!
An' thist as she kicked her heels, an' turn't to run an' hide,
They wuz two great big Black Things a-standin' by her side,
An' they snatched her through the ceilin' 'fore she knowed what she's about!
An' the Gobble-uns 'll git you
         Ef you
            Don't
               Watch
                  Out!

JANE WATSON HOPPING

An' little Orphant Annie says, when the blaze is blue,
An' the lamp-wick sputters, an' the wind goes *woo-oo!*
An' you hear the crickets quit, an' the moon is gray,
An' the lightnin'-bugs in dew is all squenched away,—
You better mind yer parunts, an' yer teachurs fond an' dear,
An' churish them 'at loves you, an' dry the orphant's tear,
An' he'p the pore an' needy ones 'at clusters all about,
Er the Gobble-uns 'll git you

Ef you

Don't

Watch

Out!

—James Whitcomb Riley
(Complete Works)

*A*DA'S TOASTED ENGLISH WALNUTS

makes 1 quart toasted nuts

To the south of Ada's barn there were several ancient walnut trees. Each year they picked a hundred pounds off the ground after the rains began in October. On cold evenings, the family would sit around the table cracking out walnuts. Ada toasted most of them and sealed them tightly in canning jars.

2 quarts boiling water   1 quart English walnuts
1 teaspoon salt

Preheat oven to 350°F. Set out a large ungreased baking sheet. Bring water to a gentle boil. Add salt and nuts and boil 3 minutes. Drain well and spread evenly on baking sheet. Toast nutmeats until golden brown, stirring often, 12 to 15 minutes. Turn out onto brown paper and let cool. Store in airtight containers.

Note: Nuts may be prepared in any quantity desired.

DELICIOUS GLAZED HAM BALLS IN A NOODLE RING

makes 6 servings

THIS IS A GOOD dish to make with leftover ham. Aunt Fanny made it often for company.

½ pound lean ham, ground
¾ pound lean pork, ground
⅔ cup dry quick-cooking oats
1 egg, beaten

½ cup milk
Glaze (recipe follows)
Noodle Ring (recipe follows)

Preheat oven to 325°F. Lightly grease shallow 12 × 7 × 2-inch baking pan; set aside until needed.

In a medium bowl, combine ham, pork, oats, egg, and milk. Mix until thoroughly blended. Chill. Shape into balls a bit larger than an egg and place in prepared pan. Bake until richly colored, about 45 to 50 minutes.

Meanwhile make Glaze: When ham balls are done, drain off fat and return to oven. Pour glaze over ham balls, reserving 2 tablespoons for noodles, and continue baking for 15 minutes more. Serve in Noodle Ring.

GLAZE

makes about one cup

⅓ cup firmly packed brown sugar
2 tablespoons cornstarch
1 teaspoon dry mustard
⅔ cup fruit juice (orange,
    pineapple, or another) or water

2 tablespoons cider vinegar
6 whole cloves
⅓ cup dark corn syrup

In a small saucepan, combine sugar, cornstarch, mustard, fruit juice, and vinegar. Add cloves and corn syrup. Cook over medium heat until slightly thickened; remove from heat and use as instructed in recipe.

NOODLE RING

makes enough noodles for 6 servings

1 pound noodles
3 eggs, well beaten
1 cup milk
⅛ teaspoon salt
⅛ teaspoon black pepper

¼ cup grated cheese, Swiss or
    Cheddar as preferred
Worcestershire sauce
2 tablespoons reserved glaze

Cook noodles and drain. Combine with egg, milk, salt, pepper, cheese, and Worcestershire sauce. Pour into buttered ring mold. Set the filled mold into a pan of hot water and bake until noodles are lightly colored and firm, about 45 minutes.

Remove noodle ring from oven, let set 5 minutes, then unmold carefully onto a large platter (round if you have one). Brush top with the reserved 2 tablespoons glaze.

CRUNCHY D'ANJOU PEAR SALAD

makes 6 salads

THE D'ANJOU IS A large, creamy yellow-green pear that keeps well in winter storage, retaining its excellent flavor throughout the season.

Crisp salad greens
6 fresh firm-ripe pears
2 tablespoons lemon juice, strained
1½ cups chopped celery (use white center stalks)

½ cup slivered almonds
½ cup mayonnaise
12 large pitted ripe olives
12 one-ounce slices Swiss cheese

Set out 6 salad plates and line them with salad greens.

Halve pears, core, and sprinkle with lemon juice; set aside while you make the filling. In a medium bowl, combine celery, almonds, and mayonnaise. Fill the pear halves with celery mixture. Place 2 pear halves on each of the prepared salad plates. Place 2 black olives on the greens at the base of each pear. Lay cheese beside them.

JANE WATSON HOPPING

$\mathcal{E}$FFIE'S COCONUT-CUSTARD PIE

makes one 9-inch pie

NONE OF US EVER knew for sure where Effie got this recipe. We all thought it must have been a prizewinner she brought back from the county fair.

Butter-Crust Pastry (page 236)
1 egg white
5 whole eggs
⅝ cup powdered sugar
2 teaspoons vanilla extract

½ teaspoon salt
2 cups milk
½ cup heavy cream
1¾ cups (¼ pound) shredded moist
    coconut

Make pastry and line a 9-inch pie tin with it before you prepare the filling. Brush the bottom of the unbaked shell with egg white and refrigerate to chill. Preheat oven to 450°F.

Into a large bowl, break *5 eggs* and stir lightly (don't beat them). Add sugar, vanilla, and salt. Pour in milk and then cream. Gently stir together. Arrange coconut in the pie shell and strain custard over it.

Bake in a hot oven for 10 minutes, then reduce heat to 350°F and bake until a knife comes out almost clean, about 20 minutes longer (do not overbake as custards continue to cook for a short time after they are removed from the oven).

Nuts, Squirrels, and Pecan Pie

From HARVEST OF THE SQUIRREL AND HONEYBEE

OH, busy squirrel with shining eyes,
And bushy tail so round,
Why do you gather all the nuts,
Which fall upon the ground?

I must prepare for winter's cold,
My harvest I must reap,
For when Jack Frost the forest claims,
Within my hole I keep.

—Alice C. D. Riley

Every fall, when the nuts are on the ground, we see gray squirrels all over, raiding the walnut orchard and the great oaks along the creek. Unusually graceful, quick, and active, they carry their silver tails over their backs, puff their cheeks with nuts or acorns, and become the center of interest. All of us drop what we are doing to watch one of them fight off a flock of bluejays that would love to move in on their gathering territory.

The silvery gray squirrels are hoarders of the most miserly kind; their stashes can be seen all about the farm. One had a large cache of nuts under the timbers of the barn. A rat much larger than the squirrel tried to take the winter's hoard, and the battle was on. That fierce squirrel sent the rat limping from the barn.

JANE WATSON HOPPING

SLIVERED ALMONDS AND DRIED-APRICOT NUT BREAD

makes one loaf

THIS LOAF IS AN excellent one for serving with hot tea and warm friendly conversation.

1½ cups dried apricots
1 cup water
1½ cups sugar
1 egg
½ cup buttermilk
2 tablespoons butter or margarine, melted

2½ cups sifted all-purpose flour
½ teaspoon salt
1 tablespoon baking powder
½ teaspoon baking soda
½ cup slivered almonds

In a medium saucepan, stew apricots with water and *½ cup sugar*. When fruit is tender, drain, saving *½ cup juice;* force fruit through a sieve. Cool.

Meanwhile, preheat oven to 350°F. Thoroughly grease a 8½ × 4½ × 2½-inch loaf pan; set aside.

In a large bowl, beat egg, milk, apricot juice, and melted butter. Add cooled fruit pulp and blend thoroughly. Into a medium bowl, sift flour with salt, baking powder, soda, and remaining *1 cup sugar*. Add egg mixture to flour mixture and blend. Then add nuts, stirring only enough to blend in.

Turn dough into prepared pan. Bake until well risen, golden brown, and firm to the touch, about 50 to 60 minutes. When done, remove from oven; let set 10 minutes. Invert bread onto a wire rack to cool, turning over so the top side is up. When cool, wrap in waxed paper or foil (flavor and texture improves when mellowed overnight).

MOTHER'S BAKED APPLE PUDDING WITH TOASTED ENGLISH WALNUTS AND BRANDY SAUCE

makes 8 servings

GRANDPA'S WALNUT GROVE YIELDED bags of large tan-colored nuts, which he sold, gave away, and used himself in great quantities. He taught me to crack them so they would yield almost 100 percent halves: Turn the pointed end up, give them a hard tap on that end with the hammer, and they crack open easily.

Mother loved to put the walnuts in her cookies, breads, and even in puddings.

⅓ cup butter or margarine,
    softened at room temperature
1 cup sugar
1 egg, beaten
1 cup sifted all-purpose flour
1 teaspoon baking soda
¼ teaspoon salt
¼ teaspoon ground cinnamon

¼ teaspoon freshly grated nutmeg
1 teaspoon vanilla extract
2 cups grated unpeeled apples
    (Jonathan preferred)
½ cup Ada's Toasted English
    Walnuts (page 227), chopped
Brandy Sauce (recipe follows)

Preheat oven to 350°F. Lightly grease an 8-inch square cake pan. Set aside.

In a large bowl, cream butter and sugar until light. Add egg and beat well. In a medium bowl, combine flour, soda, salt, cinnamon, and nutmeg; stir to blend, then add to butter mixture and combine. Finally, add vanilla, apples, and walnuts and stir together. Pour into prepared pan.

Bake until done (until cake is golden brown and springs back when touched, about 35 minutes). Serve warm or cold with a dollop of Brandy Sauce.

$\mathcal{B}$RANDY SAUCE

makes about ½ cup sauce

¼ cup butter or margarine,
    softened at room temperature
1 cup powdered sugar
1 teaspoon hot water

1 tablespoon brandy
A few grains of salt, less than
    ⅛ teaspoon

In a small bowl, beat butter and powdered sugar until smooth. Add water, brandy, and salt; beat until light.

$\mathcal{E}$ASY-TO-MAKE PECAN PIE
WITH BUTTER-CRUST PASTRY

makes about 8 servings

LIKE TURKEY AND CORN pudding, the *pacan* nut was a staple in the diet of many native American Indians long before white settlers arrived.

The stately native trees grew wild from Illinois to the Gulf. Large forests lined the riverbanks of the lower Mississippi valley. Those uncultivated, or unimproved, trees yielded small nuts with hard shells, but even so, their nuts were rich in vitamins and minerals and provided an excellent source of protein.

Butter-Crust Pastry (recipe follows)
1 cup pecan halves
3 eggs, beaten
½ cup sugar

1 cup dark corn syrup
¼ teaspoon salt
1 teaspoon vanilla extract
¼ cup butter or margarine, melted

Prepare pastry and line a 9-inch pie tin. Preheat oven to 375°F.

Spread nuts over bottom of uncooked pastry shell. In a medium bowl, combine eggs, sugar, corn syrup, salt, vanilla, and melted butter. Stir until well blended. Then, pour over pecans. Bake until the filling appears set when the pie is gently moved, 35 to 40 minutes.

When done, remove from oven. Set on a wire rack to cool.

$\mathcal{B}$UTTER-CRUST PASTRY

makes one 9-inch pie shell

1 cup all-purpose flour, plus flour
    for rolling out dough
½ teaspoon salt

½ cup cold butter
2 to 4 tablespoons cold water

Sift the flour and salt together in a large bowl. Cut the butter in, using a pastry blender or two dinner knives, or rub butter into the flour with your fingertips until all pieces of dough are the size of small peas. Gradually sprinkle over flour mixture just enough water to hold pastry together, mixing lightly and quickly with a fork after each addition. (This leads to a flakier pie crust.) Turn onto a floured surface and form into a ball (it will be soft). Chill until needed.

THANKSGIVING

LET us be thankful—not alone because
    Since last our universal thanks were told
We have grown greater in the world's applause,
    And fortune's newer smiles surpass the old—

But thankful for all things that come as alms
    From out the open hand of Providence:—
The winter clouds and storms—the summer calms—
    The sleepless dread—the drowse of indolence.

Let us be thankful—thankful for the prayers
    Whose gracious answers were long, long delayed,
That they might fall upon us unawares,
    And bless us, as in greater need we prayed.

Let us be thankful for the loyal hand
    That love held out in welcome to our own,
When love and *only* love could understand
    The need of touches we had never known.

—James Whitcomb Riley

JANE WATSON HOPPING

From Out the Open Hand of Providence

THE VERY MENTION OF Thanksgiving calls up memories of old farmhouse kitchens and pantries crowded with good things to eat.

Our friend Ada recalls the laughter and joy of having brothers, sister, children, and grandchildren, new babies and old folks, aunties and uncles all at home again, and how the greetings would fly as kinfolks arrived from long distances.

Echoes of laughter rang round the long old table with its twelve chairs as all the grown children found their old places waiting for them. Ada's father sat at the head of the table, her mother at the foot. Each year their hair became sprinkled with a bit more gray, to signal the passage of time, but each year, too the conversation was open, frank, as though it had been picked up from some other time with no break in it at all.

How grateful and glad they all were to be among those they loved, to share their triumphs and tragedies, feeling as safe and secure as they had when they were children. Through the rooms, they could hear familiar voices ringing out in long-remembered songs, and laughter bursting out when the harmony was off key. Thanksgiving was truly a time for giving thanks.

A Circle at the Fireside

WHEN I WAS GROWING up women stitched pieces of deep wisdom on samplers, things like HOME SWEET HOME and THE HOME IS THE CORNERSTONE OF CIVILIZA-TION.

From THE STICK-TOGETHER FAMILIES

THE stick-together families are happier by far
Than the brothers and the sisters who take separate highways are.
The gladdest people living are the wholesome folks who make
A circle at the fireside that no power but death can break.
And the finest of conventions ever held beneath the sun
Are the little family gatherings when the busy day is done.

It's the stick-together family that wins the joys of earth,
That hears the sweetest music and that finds the finest mirth;
It's the old home roof that shelters all the charm that life can give;
There you find the gladdest play-ground, there the happiest spot to live.
And, O weary, wandering brother, if contentment you would win,
Come you back unto the fireside and be comrade with your kin.

—Edgar A. Guest

JANE WATSON HOPPING

OUR FAMILY WAS VERY close. As Mother often said, "We loved each other in spite of shortcomings, of faults." And we stood together through thick and thin, giving and taking physical and emotional support when it was needed.

My aunt and uncles, parents and grandparents, my old warriors, as I sometimes called them when I was young, were tough and resilient. They could be difficult to deal with, willful, short-tempered and sharp-tongued, but more important was their straightforward simplicity and the vitality of their loving natures.

From them I learned that anything anyone else could do, I could do, or at least I could give it my best try, and I learned not to take myself too seriously. None of them were too dignified to race you—on the spur of the moment—uphill, and amid laughter and lots of shouting would try to beat you if they could. Each in his own way was a cutup, laughing easily at both that which was funny and that which was tragic. It was they who taught me that laughter is powerful medicine; that when you laugh, the world laughs with you, when you cry you cry alone.

None of us worry much about boredom because we all learned to create our own fun. Everyone in the family, old and young alike loves to play games, do crafts, work on personal projects. All love music, dancing, and poetry. We enjoy being together, any occasion will do—a picnic, ice cream social, family reunion, a birthday party, and of course holidays like Thanksgiving.

THE COUNTRY MOTHERS COOKBOOK

GRANDMA MEEKINS'S MOIST-ROASTED BOSTON BUTT

makes about 8 servings

THIS PIECE OF HAM may be baked like a whole ham, but Auntie liked it better moist-roasted. She and Uncle Bud often provided half a dozen such pieces of meat for a Thanksgiving dinner and made enough Raisin-Nut Sauce to serve about fifty people.

One 3- to 5-pound Boston butt
1 cup apple cider

8 sweet potatoes
Raisin-Nut Sauce (recipe follows)

Preheat oven to 350°F. Trim excess fat off the ham. Set out a covered roast pan.

Place ham in roast pan and pour apple cider around it. Bake covered until a meat thermometer reads 160°F, about 28 minutes per pound of ham. During the last half hour of the baking time, peel and halve sweet potatoes and arrange around the base of the meat.

When ham is cooked through and potatoes are tender-done, with two carving forks remove ham from pan and place on a hot serving platter. With a slotted spoon transfer sweet potatoes, laying them on the platter around the ham. Serve the sweet potatoes first, then carve ham and place a slice on each person's plate. *Note:* When ham is carved in the kitchen the sweet potatoes may be served in a separate dish or may be laid around the carved ham. Either way serve piping hot with Raisin-Nut Sauce on the side.

NOTE: Let drippings cool in roast pan. When fat has firmed up, remove from the congealed drippings and freeze drippings for flavoring beans or split pea soup.

RAISIN-NUT SAUCE

makes about 2¾ cups

1 cup dark or light raisins
2 cups apple cider
¼ tablespoon cornstarch

2 tablespoons butter
½ cup Toasted Pecans (recipe
    follows)

In a medium saucepan soak raisins in cider to reconstitute. Heat to boiling, then boil 1 minute. Moisten the cornstarch with water, stir into sauce and continue cooking until sauce is thick. Stir in butter until melted and blended. Just before serving with ham, fold in nuts.

TOASTED PECANS

makes ½ cup

GRANDPA LOVED PECANS, RAW or toasted. When he was a boy he gathered them in the bottomlands. When I was small, he would have a few in glass jars in his bedroom, and would share some with me, making for cookies and special recipes.

1 pint boiling water
1 teaspoon salt

½ cup shelled pecans

Preheat oven to 350°F. Set out a large ungreased baking sheet. Bring water to a gentle boil. Add salt and nuts and boil 3 minutes. Drain well and spread evenly on baking sheet. Toast nutmeats until lightly browned, stirring often, 12 to 15 minutes. Turn out onto brown paper, use immediately in Raisin-Nut Sauce, or cool thoroughly and store in an airtight container for later use.

$\mathcal{V}$ERA'S PAN-FRIED PARSNIPS

makes 6 servings

THE KAMPINGS HAVE ALWAYS had lovely gardens. They plant parsnips in early spring as soon as the ground can be worked. When they are a little larger than big carrots, Vera pulls some and leaves the rest in the ground to grow larger through the fall and even through the winter. When left in the ground to winter over, parsnips may be dug anytime the ground thaws. By spring they are often huge with side roots on them—surprising enough, they may still be tender and mild.

Vera appreciates them most during a mild winter, as she can dig them at will and pan-fry them for supper.

3 tablespoons bacon grease
   (another fat may be substituted)
6 small raw parsnips, peeled and
   sliced

½ teaspoon salt
¼ teaspoon black pepper
3 tablespoons cold water

Heat bacon grease in a large frying pan over high heat, then add parsnips. Turn down the heat to low and stir-fry until the parsnips begin to brown. Add salt and pepper. Pour the water into the pan, cover, and steam until parsnips are tender-done and the water is gone. Lift the lid. If the parsnips do not seem done, add a little more water and continue steaming.

JANE WATSON HOPPING

CORNMEAL EGG BREAD

makes 2 loaves of bread

THIS BREAD MAKES VERY good French toast. Will Bates smeared gobs of butter on his.

2 tablespoons granulated yeast
¼ cup lukewarm water
2 cups milk
¼ cup sugar
1 tablespoon salt

½ cup butter or margarine
1 cup cornmeal
2 eggs, well beaten
5 to 6 cups unbleached all-purpose
    flour, plus 1 cup for kneading

In a small bowl, put yeast in lukewarm water to soften.

In a medium saucepan, scald the milk. While it is still hot, add sugar, salt, and butter. Stir until sugar and salt are dissolved and the butter has melted. Into a very large bowl, put cornmeal. Pour the hot milk mixture over it and stir until meal is moistened. Let the mixture cool to lukewarm.

Then add the yeast, eggs, and about *3 cups* of the flour. Set the sponge (batter) in a warm place to rise. When double in bulk, add the *remaining* flour. Stir until a medium-stiff dough is formed (one that can be handled without sticking to the hands). Turn out onto a floured flat surface. Knead until dough is elastic, adding additional flour as needed. Wash the mixing bowl in hot water, scald and dry it. Grease it, then put the ball of dough into the bowl, turning it about until the ball of dough is greased. Then cover with a clean cloth and set aside to rise.

When dough has doubled in bulk, punch it down, but not too hard. Turn out onto the floured surface again, divide in half, and shape into loaves. Grease two 4 × 8-inch loaf pans. Put the loaves into the pans, turning the dough over so as to grease the top (make sure the pinched or sealed side is down for baking). Set to rise until double in bulk.

Meanwhile, preheat oven to 400°F. Bake loaves for 20 minutes, then turn the temperature down to 350°F and continue baking until the bread is golden brown, 35 to 40 minutes more. When bread is done, remove from the oven and turn out of the pans (loosening gently with a table knife if necessary). Set on wire racks to cool.

ADA'S DEEP-DISH PEAR PIE

makes about 6 servings

SOME WINTER-KEEPING PEARS ARE SO sweet they may be baked into pie without sugar added. Such are the D'Anjous, which keep well in storage and retain their excellent sweet flavor. Ada thought this variety could not be beaten for making pie, especially a deep-dish pie.

Butter-Crust Pastry (page 236)
5 cups peeled, cored, and sliced
    pears (D'Anjous preferred)
Juice of 1 lemon, strained
1 cup sugar, or less (about ½ cup)
    if pears are very sweet

½ teaspoon salt
1 tablespoon tapioca
2 tablespoons butter, softened at
    room temperature
Chilled heavy cream (optional)

Preheat oven to 425°F. Make pastry and chill until needed.

In a large, flat 9 × 12-inch baking dish layer pears with lemon juice, sugar, salt, and tapioca and stir gently to blend. Dot butter over the top.

Remove the pastry from the refrigerator. Turn it out onto a lightly floured surface. Roll out the pastry into a shape that will completely cover the dish, then fit it over the top of the baking dish, trim and crimp as desired. Cut vent holes in the top and bake until the crust is golden brown and the pears are tender when pierced with a skewer, about 45 minutes. Serve hot or cold, with or without chilled heavy cream spooned over it.

JANE WATSON HOPPING

Grandpa's Birthday

ASIDE FROM CHRISTMAS, GRANDPA'S birthday was the biggest holiday of the year, because it was not only a day to celebrate his passing years, but the day on which the family restocked his supplies for the year. Born before the turn of the century, he had no pension, but country-proud, he and his children would have died before they took charity for his care; staunchly they maintained that "kinfolk took care of their own."

Thus the month-long checking and conferences as Uncle Arch, Aunt Mabel, and Mother—for the most part—helped Grandpa look over his things to see what he needed. Then they all got together and figured out the cost and made more lists. Grandpa's needs were never great—tobacco, wool blankets, underwear, shirts and overalls, coffee, some fishing gear, a new shovel—but you would never have guessed so by the excitement afoot.

Then, of course, there was the birthday party to get ready for: cakes to bake, his favorite dishes to prepare, tables to set, and presents to wrap. Soon the family would all be gathered for the festivities. There was never room enough at the tables, but we children never had to wait until the grownups were through eating, as many children did in those days. Our plates were filled and our milk was poured and we were invited to sit on cushions on the floor around a makeshift table, which was covered with a crisp clean cloth.

Today when we gather, we talk about those times, the good food and family, and I must admit that it brings up memories that are so dear that they are painful.

THE COUNTRY MOTHERS COOKBOOK

SOUTHERN SMOTHERED RABBIT WITH DOWN-HOME BEATEN BISCUITS AND HOMEMADE BUTTER

makes about 6 servings

A BIT OF SOUTHERN comfort, this tender oven-cooked rabbit begs for milk gravy and beaten biscuits. In our family, a little fresh butter was churned for the biscuits and a dish of black-eyed peas was served on the side.

½ cup all-purpose flour
1 teaspoon salt
½ teaspoon black pepper
¼ teaspoon dried thyme leaves, pulverized
3-pound young rabbit, cut into serving pieces

About 3 tablespoons butter, margarine, or oil
½ cup hot water
Milk Gravy (recipe follows)
Down-Home Beaten Biscuits (recipe follows)
Homemade Butter (page 89)

Preheat oven to 350°F. Lightly grease a 2-quart baking dish with a cover.

In a brown paper bag, combine flour, salt, black pepper, and thyme; shake to blend. Then add the rabbit pieces a few at a time and shake well to coat. In a heavy skillet, heat butter until melted and skillet is hot. Cook rabbit pieces until browned and then put them in the prepared baking dish. When all pieces are browned, pour hot water around the base of the meat. Cover the dish tightly and bake until meat is tender, about 1 hour.

Remove from oven. Lift the rabbit out of the baking dish and keep warm. Make Milk Gravy.

JANE WATSON HOPPING

$\mathcal{M}$ILK GRAVY

makes about 6 servings

Drippings   2 cups milk
3 rounded tablespoons flour

Pour off all but about 4 tablespoons from dish drippings. Scrape residue and drippings into a skillet; stir in flour and blend. Let flour cook and brown a little in the fat (don't let it burn). When flour is brown, pour milk into the skillet; stir constantly until gravy has thickened. Serve immediately with rabbit and over hot biscuits.

$\mathcal{D}$OWN-HOME BEATEN BISCUITS

makes 10 to 12 biscuits

THESE BISCUITS ARE MORE work than quick buttermilk biscuits, but Mother would make them to please the two men she loved most in life—her husband and father.

2 cups flour   ½ cup cold butter or margarine
½ teaspoon salt   ⅓ cup water
1 tablespoon sugar

Preheat oven to 400°F. Grease a cookie sheet.

Sift flour with salt and sugar. Cut in butter and then add water. Mix into a very stiff dough. Turn out onto a floured bread board. Beat with a rolling pin or a potato masher for 3 minutes to develop the gluten. (In the South, where these biscuits are popular, there is a saying: "300 strokes for everyday biscuits, 500 strokes for company.") Fold edges in after each stroke. Roll out ⅓ inch thick and cut with a biscuit cutter. Prick the top of each biscuit with a fork and bake on a greased cookie sheet for about 20 minutes, or until they are browned.

THE TOUCH OF LOVING HANDS

LIGHT falls the rain-drop on the fallen leaf,
    And light o'er harvest-plain and garnered sheaf—
    But lightlier falls the touch of loving hands.

Light falls the dusk of mild midsummer night,
And light the first star's faltering lance of light
    On glimmering lawns,—but lightlier loving hands.

And light the feathery flake of early snows,
Or wisp of thistle-down that no wind blows,
    And light the dew,—but lightlier loving hands.

Light-falling dusk, or dew, or summer rain,
Or down of snow or thistle—all are vain,—
    For lightlier falls the touch of loving hands.

—James Whitcomb Riley

GRANDMA MEEKINS'S
MASHED-POTATO SALAD

makes 6 to 8 servings

THIS IS A FAVORITE potato salad that we think must have come from Grandma Meekins, since it is tart and was written on a ragged piece of paper in her "doctor book."

6 medium potatoes, peeled, quartered, boiled, and mashed (cover to keep warm)
6 hard-cooked eggs, shelled and chopped
1 cup chopped dill pickles
½ cup chopped sweet onion
2 rounded tablespoons prepared mustard

⅓ cup cider vinegar
⅔ cup mayonnaise
1½ teaspoons salt
Sprig of fresh parsley, finely minced
Dash of paprika (less than ⅛ teaspoon)

While still hot, put mashed potatoes in a large bowl; add the eggs, pickles, and onion. In a small bowl, combine mustard, vinegar, mayonnaise, and salt. Spoon over potato mixture and stir until blended. (The salad should have the consistency of light mashed potatoes; if too thick, thin with a little pickle juice.) Sprinkle on minced parsley and a dash of paprika.

GRANDPA'S FAVORITE
CHICKEN-FRIED OYSTERS

makes 4 servings

2 eggs
¼ teaspoon salt
¼ teaspoon pepper
⅓ cup heavy cream
⅓ cup oyster liquid
2 jars medium-large drained oysters

⅔ cup flour
1½ cups fine dry bread crumbs or
  cracker crumbs
Butter or margarine for frying

Beat the eggs, add salt, pepper, cream, and oyster liquid, and beat again. Dip the oysters first into the liquid, then into the flour, back into the liquid, then roll in bread crumbs or cracker meal. Fry in butter or margarine until the coating is light brown. If more oysters than will fit in the pan at one time are to be fried, use a clean pan and new butter. (Butter burns quickly and so does cracker meal.) Be sure not to scorch the oysters, as their delicate flavor will be ruined.

A DAKOTA WHEAT FIELD

BROAD as the fleckless, soaring sky
  Mysterious, fair as the moon-led sea
The vast plain flames on the dazzled eye
  Under the fierce sun's alchemy.
    The slow hawk stoops
      To his prey in the deeps;
    The sunflower droops
      To the lazy wave; the wind sleeps.
Then all in dazzling links and loops,
  A riot of shadow and shine,
  A glory of olive and amber and wine,
To the westering sun the colors run
Through the deeps of the ripening wheat.

—Hamlin Garland

JANE WATSON HOPPING

AUNT MAE'S EGGLESS GINGERBREAD

makes 4 to 6 servings

THIS ANTIQUE WINTER-TIME RECIPE came out of Aunt Mae's handwritten cookbook.

1 cup apple jelly
⅓ cup butter
¼ cup firmly packed light brown
    sugar
¾ cup buttermilk
2½ cups sifted all-purpose flour
1 tablespoon ground ginger

1 teaspoon ground cinnamon
1 teaspoon baking soda
1 tablespoon unsweetened
    powdered cocoa
½ teaspoon salt
Sweetened Whipped Cream (page
    17), optional

Preheat oven to 350°F. Thoroughly grease a 5 × 9 × 3-inch loaf pan.

In a large saucepan, over low heat, put jelly, butter, and brown sugar to warm. When butter is melted and sugar dissolved, remove from heat, cover, and keep warm. Measure buttermilk and set aside. Sift flour with ginger, cinnamon, soda, cocoa, and salt. To the warmed jelly butter mixture in the pan, add flour mixture alternately with buttermilk. Stir just enough to blend well. Pour into prepared pan.

Bake until well risen, browned, and light to the touch, 40 to 45 minutes. Remove from oven and cool in the pan. Serve plain or with Sweetened Whipped Cream.

$\mathcal{L}$EMON MERINGUE PIE

makes one 9-inch pie, about 6 to 8 servings

AUNT MABEL MADE LOVELY lemon pies mounded with meringue, on which beads of glistening sweetness clung. Just about everybody in the family would ask her to bring lemon pie to a family gathering.

Butter-Crust Pastry (page 236) | 2½ cups boiling water
1 cup sugar | 3 egg yolks
½ cup all-purpose flour | 3 tablespoons grated lemon rind
2 tablespoons cornstarch | 6 tablespoons lemon juice, strained
½ teaspoon salt | Meringue (recipe follows)

Preheat oven to 400°F. Make pastry and roll out about ⅛ inch thick. Line a 9-inch pie pan and prick the crust so it won't puff. Trim and crimp edge. Bake shell until light brown; set aside to cool.

Reduce oven temperature to 375°F. In the top of a heated double boiler, combine *¾ cup sugar,* flour, cornstarch, and salt. Slowly add boiling water, stirring constantly to keep the filling smooth. Cook over boiling water until thick enough to mound when dropped from a spoon; stir constantly. Cover and cook 10 minutes more.

Beat egg yolks; add remaining *¼ cup sugar* to them and beat again. When the filling has cooked, pour some of it over the egg yolks, stirring constantly. When thoroughly blended, add the yolk-filling mixture to the rest of the filling in the pan. Cook over boiling water about 5 minutes, stirring constantly. Remove from heat and stir in lemon rind and juice. Mix well and let cool. When cooled, spoon the filling into the shell. Make meringue. Pile meringue on the cooled pie filling and spread it over the pie, taking care that it touches the shell. Using a teaspoon, swirl the top of the meringue leaving high and low surfaces. Peaks should not be too high as they tend to get overly brown before the rest of the meringue has turned golden.

Bake 10 minutes, or until golden-tan. Cool away from drafts.

MERINGUE

3 egg whites (from eggs used in
    filling)
¼ teaspoon salt

½ teaspoon vanilla extract
6 tablespoons granulated sugar

Place egg whites in a large bowl. Add salt and vanilla and beat into rounded peaks. Add sugar, *1 tablespoon* at a time, beating until meringue is stiff and glossy but not dry.

LEMON PIE

THE world is full of gladness,
    There are joys of many kinds,
There's a cure for every sadness,
    That each troubled mortal finds.
And my little cares grow lighter
    And I cease to fret and sigh,
And my eyes with joy grow brighter
    When she makes a lemon pie.

When the bronze is on the filling
    That's one mass of shining gold,
And its molten joy is spilling
    On the plate, my heart grows bold
And the kids and I in chorus
    Raise one glad exultant cry
And we cheer the treat before us—
    Which is mother's lemon pie.

Then the little troubles vanish,
    And the sorrows disappear,
Then we find the grit to banish
    All the cares that hovered near,
And we smack our lips in pleasure
    O'er a joy no coin can buy,
And we down the golden treasure
    Which is known as lemon pie.

—Edgar A. Guest

JANE WATSON HOPPING

254

Hurrah for the Fun! — Is the Pudding Done?

ADA WAS ONE OF those women whose yard was always full of children. When her own were growing up, their overnight guests—and there were many of them—always slept in her great loft upstairs. When she became a grandmother, all the children that ever passed through her door called her Nana, and she received more grimy hugs, wild flower bouquets, and colorful wild bird feathers than anyone we ever knew:

> *Over the river and through the wood*
> *Now Grandmother's cap I spy:*
> *Hurrah for the fun!—Is the pudding done?*
> *Hurrah for the pumpkin-pie!*
>
> —School Reader

The Schoolboy's Favorite

FER any boy 'at's little as me,
    Er any little girl,
That-un's the goodest poetry piece
    In any book in the worl'!
An' ef grown-peoples wuz little ag'in
    I bet they'd say so, too,
Ef *they'd* go see *their* ole Gran'ma,
    Like our Pa lets *us* do!

Over the river an' through the wood
    Now Gran'mother's cap I spy:
Hurrah fer the fun!—Is the puddin' done?—
    Hurrah fer the punkin-pie!

An' 'll tell *you* why 'at's the goodest piece:—
    'Cause it's ist like *we* go
To *our* Gran'ma's, a-visitun there,
    When our Pa he says so;
An' Ma she fixes my little cape-coat
    An' little fuzz-cap; an' Pa
He tucks me away—an' yells *"Hoor-ray!"*—
An' whacks Ole Gray, an' drives the sleigh
    Fastest you ever saw!

Over the river an' through the wood
    Now Gran'mother's cap I spy:
Hurrah fer the fun! Is the puddin' done?—
    Hurrah fer the punkin-pie!

An' Pa ist snuggles me 'tween his knees—
    An' I he'p hold the lines,
An' peek out over the buffalo-robe;—
An' the wind ist *blows!*—an' the snow ist *snows!*
    An' the sun ist shines! an' shines!—
An' th' ole horse tosses his head an' coughs
    The frost back in our face.—
An' I' ruther go to my Gran'ma's
    Than any other place!

Over the river an' through the wood
    Now Gran'mother's cap I spy:
Hurrah fer the fun!—Is the puddin' done?—
    Hurrah fer the punkin-pie!

An' all the peoples they is in town
    Watches us whizzin' past
To go a-visitun *our* Gran'ma's,
    Like we all went there last;—

But *they* can't go, like ist *our* folks
    An' Johnny an' Lotty, and three
Er four neighbor-childerns, an' Rober-ut Volney
    An' Charley an' Maggy an' me!

Over the river an' through the wood
    Now Gran'mother's cap I spy:
Hurrah fer the fun!—Is the puddin' done?—
    Hurrah fer the punkin-pie!

—James Whitcomb R

Hurrah for the Punkin Pie!

ALL THROUGH THE HOLIDAY season from Thanksgiving until Christmas, Mother worked on the "gift packages." She made colorful pot holders on the sewing machine out of remnants from our dresses, and crocheted others that were lovely and fit only for hanging up to decorate the kitchen. She made doilies for older women in the community who could no longer crochet. And she baked endless piles of cookies and loaves of bread. Our favorites were sweet breads and homemade yeast breads of every ilk.

When she had all of her goodies piled on the table, she would pack them carefully among polished red, green, and striped apples, homemade muslin bags full of walnuts and almonds. At the last minute, she would bake several pumpkin pies, and would gingerly put them, when cooled, on top of her box, along with a batch of homemade candy, fudge, peanut brittle, or divinity.

Then we would help her distribute them. Sometimes the younger women widows or maiden ladies would have presents for us to take home. My favorite memory is receiving a white lawn handkerchief with finely wrought hand-tatted lace on it, which I kept in a miniature cedar chest for years.

THE COUNTRY MOTHERS COOKBOOK

GRANDMA'S PUMPKIN CUSTARD PIE WITH GRAHAM CRACKER CRUMB TOPPING

makes one 9-inch pie

THIS PIE CHANGED WITH Grandma's moods—one time it would have a vanilla wafer topping, sometimes a homemade cookie crumb crust. However she made it, no one ever refused a slice of her pumpkin custard pie.

Butter-Crust Pastry (page 236)
2 eggs, beaten to a froth
1½ cups fresh pureed or canned
    pumpkin
⅓ cup light brown sugar
1½ teaspoons ground cinnamon
¼ teaspoon freshly ground nutmeg

¼ teaspoon ground ginger
½ teaspoon salt
1 cup evaporated milk
¼ cup water
⅓ cup apricot jam
Graham Cracker Topping (recipe
    follows)

Make pastry and chill. Just before preparing the filling, roll out the pastry and line a 9-inch pie pan; set aside until needed. Preheat oven to 350°F.

In a medium bowl, combine beaten eggs, pumpkin, brown sugar, cinnamon, nutmeg, ginger, and salt. With a wire whisk, stir to blend; then, blend in evaporated milk, water, and apricot jam. Pour into prepared pastry shell.

Bake until custard is partially cooked and crust has puffed up, about 20 minutes. Meanwhile, prepare topping.

Carefully remove pie from oven and sprinkle the crumbs evenly over its top (use the back of a spoon for spreading if needed). Return pie to oven and bake until filling shimmers just slightly when pan is gently shaken, about 30 minutes longer. Remove pie from oven; set aside to cool. (The heat in the pie will continue to cook custard and firm it up.) Serve while still warm.

GRAHAM CRACKER CRUMB TOPPING

½ cup fine graham cracker crumbs
½ cup sugar
¼ cup very finely chopped walnuts

¼ teaspoon cinnamon
About 3 tablespoons melted butter

In a small bowl, combine cracker crumbs, sugar, nuts, and cinnamon. Add melted butter and mix until crumbly.

EFFIE'S FAVORITE COCONUT COOKIES

makes 3 dozen cookies

THESE ARE LOVELY TO look at, and delicious, too. They're one of Effie's show-off cookies.

1¼ cups sifted all-purpose flour
1 teaspoon baking powder
1 teaspoon baking soda
½ teaspoon salt
½ cup granulated sugar
½ cup firmly packed light brown
    sugar

½ cup butter or margarine,
    softened at room temperature
1 egg
½ teaspoon vanilla extract
1 cup dry quick-cooking oats
1 cup flaky coconut

Preheat oven to 350°F. Lightly grease a large baking sheet.

Into a large bowl, sift flour with baking powder, soda, and salt. Add granulated and brown sugars, butter, egg, and vanilla. Beat into a smooth batter, about 2 to 3 minutes.

Fold in oats and coconut. Shape into small balls. Place on prepared baking sheet and bake until cookies spread and are lightly brown in color, 12 to 15 minutes. Remove from oven and transfer with a spatula to a piece of brown paper or a wire rack to cool. Store in an airtight container.

RISE-AND-SHINE FRUITED OATMEAL BREAD

makes one loaf

UNCLE BUD THOUGHT THIS was just what the doctor ordered for a winter-time, before-chores snack. Sometimes he would eat nearly half a loaf and swig down burning cups of strong coffee before he went out into the icy cold morning air to feed poultry and livestock, break the ice on the watering troughs, and cuss the cold.

Auntie always fussed about his filling up on her sweet bread, and she would tell him: "If you'll just wait until I can get the stove going, I'll cook you a proper breakfast,"—which meant sausage, eggs, biscuits, and milk gravy.

Even so, when the weather was nasty, she regularly made this bread, and watched constantly out of the windows on such mornings, keeping an eye on Uncle Bud's lantern light as it bobbed about in the crisp, achingly cold air of the farm yard.

1 egg	½ teaspoon salt
1 cup buttermilk	1 cup dry quick-cooking or
½ cup dark or light brown sugar,	regular oats
as preferred	1 cup chopped dates or raisins
1 cup sifted all-purpose flour	½ cup nuts (walnuts preferred)
1 teaspoon baking soda	3 tablespoons melted butter

Preheat oven to 350°F. Grease a 7¾ × 3⅝ × 2¼-inch loan pan, line the bottom with waxed paper, then grease the paper. Set aside.

In a large bowl, combine egg, buttermilk, and sugar. Into a medium bowl, sift flour with soda and salt. Add flour mixture all at once to the egg mixture, stirring only enough to blend. Add oats, dates, and nuts; stir only to blend. Fold in melted butter. Turn into prepared loaf pan.

Bake until loaf is well browned and firm to the touch, 45 to 50 minutes. When done, remove from oven, loosen with a knife blade if necessary, then turn onto a wire rack. While still hot, remove paper from bottom of the loaf. Turn right side up. Serve piping hot or cold. For cold bread, cool thoroughly, then wrap in a piece of foil or waxed paper; store in a cool, dry place for about 24 hours to mellow.

JANE WATSON HOPPING

The Joy of Giving

I shared my crust with a poorer one,
 And the crust—which had seemed but a bit of bread
When *one* would eat—was a glorious feast
 When shared with another, instead.

I shared my bed with a poorer one—
 So poor a bed, but a board or two—
But 't was soft as feathers to me, and I slept
 With a peace that I rarely knew.

I shared my joy with a poorer one,
 And lo! 't was increased to a joy divine
For another was cheered by the kindly thought,
 When they felt that joy of mine.

My gifts were poor, but were of my best,
 I had given myself when I gave my food.
But the joy that came transfigured all,
 And I felt that God was good.

For a selfish joy is an empty thing,
 Since it fades away as the passing dreams,
But the joy of giving is sweet and free,
 And ever a new joy seems.

So share your best, though it be but poor,
 With a willing heart and a spirit brave;
For a joy will come that will far outweigh
 The trifle that you gave.

—Gladys M. Adams (Age 16)

(Cash Prize)

From O' Little Town of Bethlehem

How silently, how silently
The wondrous gift is giv'n!
So God imparts to human hearts
The blessings of His heav'n.

—Phillips Brooks

JANE WATSON HOPPING

Christmas Comes But Once a Year

FOR DECADES CHRISTMAS HAS been a joyful blend of holiday spirit, reverence, and gaiety—the most exciting holiday of the year—and the season that most fills us with nostalgia. There is something about Christmas that sets it apart from other days and hallows it, something that probes the human soul, and inspires people in all walks of life to kind thoughts, good deeds, and wrongs made right.

Our mother, who loves Christmas, often told us stories of her childhood home: of decorated trees, ribbons and wreaths, and of course of the family all together, admiring the great oak table laden with ham, fresh pork roast, wintertime vegetables, mincemeat pies, apple desserts of all kinds, and pitchers of cold milk.

Sometimes she reminds us of our own Depression-era kitchen, the great wood cookstove, aunties moving among the pots and pans, some reviving favorite Christmas recipes, others following newfangled recipes.

Always, she talks about Christmas, the hush when a white-robed choir begins the songs of joy, when across the cold clean air bells proclaim Christ's birth and fills our hearts with hope for peace on earth, good will to men. And always we speak of the warmth of the spirit of Christmas, which defies the power of prose or rhyme.

THE COUNTRY MOTHERS COOKBOOK

A Rattle of Silver So Bright

WHEN SHEILA WAS A little tiny girl she loved Santa Claus, she loved everything about him from his "Ho! Ho! Ho!" to the pack on his back. She talked about him endlessly. Then when we were up town, shopping a little for Christmas (in the 1930s we did not buy a great deal), she saw a tiny baby only a few days old, and she thought, right then, that the baby needed a rattle, a bright silver one. We asked her why a silver rattle, and she told us, "Because it would shine and she wouldn't loose it."

JANE WATSON HOPPING

SONG OF THE CHILD-WORLD

DEAR Santa Claus come down the chimney tonight,
Be sure that you do not forget,
You will find us all tucked in our beds snug and tight,
Each hoping a gift to get.

Dear Mother would like a new ring—I think,
And Father a new book, you know,
While Sister just longs for a doll that can wink,
And a watch that will really go.

The Baby must have a new bonnet of blue,
And a rattle of silver so bright,
As for me, dear old Santa, I leave it up to you,
Some skates or a drum and kite.

—Alice C. D. Riley, Helen A. Lloyd, Jessie L. Gaynor
The John Church Company, 1897

THE COUNTRY MOTHERS COOKBOOK

VELVET CHOCOLATE FUDGE

makes about 2 pounds of fudge

ONCE WOMEN IN OUR family discovered the use of undiluted evaporated milk in candymaking, batches were given lavishly at Christmas and on all holidays throughout the year. Uncle Ben preferred this velvety chocolate fudge.

3 squares (3 ounces) unsweetened
    chocolate
3 cups sugar
2 tablespoons light corn syrup

1 cup evaporated milk
3 tablespoons butter or margarine
1 teaspoon vanilla extract

Butter a 9-inch square cake pan.

In a heavy-bottomed saucepan, put chocolate, sugar, corn syrup, and evaporated milk. Over medium heat, stir until chocolate melts. Cook until mixture forms a soft ball in cold water (234°F on a candy thermometer). Remove from heat. Add butter and vanilla. Allow to cool until pan is cool enough to hold on palm of hand (110°F), then beat fudge until thick and creamy. Spread in prepared pan. When firm, cut into squares.

EASY-TO-MAKE FONDANT

makes about 1 pound fondant

THIS FONDANT MAY BE used plain or filled with nuts, candied fruit, coconut, or other goodies—the variations are endless. Ada usually pressed a whole nutmeat into half of her fondant balls and candied cherries into the tops of the rest.

2 cups sugar
¼ teaspoon salt

1 tablespoon light corn syrup
1 cup evaporated milk

In a heavy-bottomed saucepan, combine sugar, salt, corn syrup, and evaporated milk. Cook over medium heat, stirring constantly, until syrup forms a medium-firm ball in cold water (240°F on a candy thermometer). Remove from heat; cool to lukewarm (110°F). Beat until thick and creamy. Place in a covered dish overnight.

The next day, form fondant into ½-inch balls; fill and decorate as desired.

NOTE: When cooking to a specific temperature, use a candy thermometer to take the guesswork out of candymaking.

PENUCHE

makes about 1½ pounds penuche

MY COUSIN JOAN LIKES to make fudge and penuche, delicious brown sugar fudge.

2 cups firmly packed brown sugar
½ teaspoon salt
2 tablespoons light corn syrup
¾ cup evaporated milk

2 tablespoons butter or margarine
1 teaspoon vanilla extract
⅔ cup chopped nuts

Butter an 8-inch square cake pan.

In a heavy-bottomed saucepan, put sugar, salt, corn syrup, and evaporated milk. Cook over medium heat, stirring constantly, until syrup forms a soft ball in cold water (234°F on a candy thermometer). Cool to lukewarm (110°F). Stir in butter, vanilla, and nuts. Beat until thick and creamy. Turn into prepared pan. Cool, then cut into squares.

Treasures from the Attic

WHEN ADA WAS A little girl, she lived in a big old farmhouse that had been in the family for generations. There were six bedrooms in it, a downstairs and upstairs, a huge basement with a coal bin, and an attic stacked high with trunks filled with keepsakes: toys, a unicycle, a great wooden rocking horse, dolls that were in their prime before the Civil War. There were small wooden boxes of family documents and chairs and pictures of the old days, everything one could imagine.

While the children could not play in the attic because of its large windows that opened out, at Christmastime they could go upstairs with their grandfather and pick out some of the toys that they best loved, bring them down and set them under the tree, and after Santa Claus came, could keep them forever.

GRANDPA'S TOY

WHEN grandpa was a little boy—
    And that 's a far-off day,
For now grandpa is very old,
    And never thinks of play—

Grandpa lived in the good old times
    When "everything was right";
They had no carpets on the floors,
    And they read by candle-light.

And his toy-horse looks very crude,
    It's tail is like a broom;
The wagon is high and funny,
    And has but little room.

But grandpa thinks it the nicest toy
    That ever yet was made;
He would not for an automobile
    This queer old wagon trade.

I suppose when *you* are grandpas
You'll think *your* toys were great
'Way back in the days when you were young;
    But *you'll* be out of date.

—Ruth Titus

JANE WATSON HOPPING

268

GRANDMA'S CHRISTMAS CAKE

makes about 12 servings

THIS OLD CAKE IS delicious when served with hot coffee. On Saturday morning all of the grandchildren in Ada's family loved to drop in because they knew she would be baking this cake for her father. If she suspected that more than three or four pushing, shoving, giggling little ones were on their way, she would make at least two cakes this size.

½ cup butter or margarine,
    softened at room temperature
2 cups sugar
2 eggs, beaten to a froth
2 cups sifted all-purpose flour
2 teaspoons soda
2 teaspoons ground cinnamon
1 teaspoon ground ginger
3 TBlS Cocoa pwd.

½ teaspoon salt
4 cups peeled, cored, and diced tart
    fresh apples (Jonathan
    preferred)
1 cup golden raisins
1 cup chopped pecans
Sweetened Whipped Cream (page
    17)

Preheat oven to 350°F. Grease and flour a 9 × 12-inch baking dish. Set aside.

In a large bowl, cream together butter, sugar, and eggs. Into a medium bowl, sift flour with soda, cinnamon, ginger, and salt. Add flour mixture to the butter-egg mixture and stir hard to blend. When thoroughly mixed, fold in apples, raisins, and nuts. Turn into prepared pan.

Bake until cake is well-risen, golden brown, and firm to the touch, about 50 minutes. Remove from oven, cool in the pan on a wire rack. Serve plain or with a dollop of Sweetened Whipped Cream.

THE COUNTRY MOTHERS COOKBOOK

Away Up in the Heather

ON COLD AFTERNOONS OR evenings when all the children were inside out of the weather, Aunt Clary used to tell them stories about her childhood and about her grandmother who had come from far across the sea to make a new life in a new land. And how the cities were so crowded and there was little honest work to be found. And how she, just a slip of a girl, had taken the last of her money and bought a ticket on the train to Ohio, the land of milk and honey, where she married her dear husband and became an American citizen.

And as Aunt Clary reminded the children, their great-great-grandmother had become the mother of a large Irish-American family, a host of sturdy boys and girls whose lives had spoken proudly of their heritage.

Not so long ago, when I first read this poem, "Grace for Light," it reminded me of those winter tales. Thus I have included it here in memory of my own immigrant ancestors and those of many other Americans who came from distant lands.

This song of the Glens of Antrim was written prior to 1904 by Moira O'Neill in the dialect of the glens, and chiefly for the pleasure of other Glens' people.

JANE WATSON HOPPING

GRACE FOR LIGHT

WHEN we were little childer we had a quare wee house,
  Away up in the heather by the head o' Brabla' burn;
The hares we'd see them scootin', an' we'd hear the crowin' grouse,
  An' when we'd all be in at night ye'd not get room to turn.

The youngest two She'd put to bed, their faces to the wall,
  An' the lave of us could sit aroun', just anywhere we might;
Herself 'ud take the rush-dip an' light it for us all,
  An' *"God be thankèd!"* she would say,—*"now we have a light."*

Then we be to quet the laughin' an' pushin' on the floor,
  An' think on One who called us to come and be forgiven;
Himself 'ud put his pipe down, an' say the good word more,
  "May the Lamb o' God lead us all to the Light o' Heaven!"

There' a wheen things that used to be an' now has had their day,
  The nine Glens of Antrim can show ye many a sight;
But not the quare wee house where we lived up Brabla' way,
  Nor a child in all the nine Glens that knows the grace for light.

—Moira O'Neill

THE COUNTRY MOTHERS COOKBOOK

271

Index

A

acorn squash: *see* squash, acorn
Adams, Gladys M., 261
Ada's cornstarch pudding (blancmange), 24
Ada's deep-dish pear pie, 244
Ada's Easter salad, 62
Ada's macaroni salad, 188
Ada's old-time strawberry shortcake, 131
Ada's toasted English walnuts, 227
Ada's two-colored cookies, 58
Aldrich, Thomas Bailey, xxviii, 124
"The All-Golden" (Riley), xxix
almond(s):
    cluster cookies, 136
    and dried-apricot nut bread, slivered, 233
    fairy-light meringues filled with slivered, 149
    in four-cup pudding, 45
    icing, 9
amethyst raspberry tarts with cookie crust tart shells, 198–99
Ann's easy-to-make star cookies, 122
apple(s):
    in Christmas cake, 269
    cookies, Arkansas black, 30
    dessert, a crowd-pleasing, 40
    dumplings, 224
    pie with tip-top pastry dough, 52–53
    pudding with toasted English walnuts and brandy sauce, baked, 234–35
    raisin cookies, 59
apricots, dried:
    and slivered almonds nut bread, 233
aspic, tomato, 63
"At Aunty's House" (Riley), 202
Aunt Clary's boiled hen with Dutch dumplings, 76–77
Aunt Clary's chicken gruel, 75
Aunt Fanny's Arkansas black apple cookies, 30

Aunt Fanny's four-cup pudding, 45
Aunt Fanny's ham salad in a scalloped watermelon boat with lemon mayonnaise dressing, 176–77
Aunt Fanny's lemon cloverleaf rolls glazed with heavy cream, 170–71
Aunt Fanny's liberty cake with lemon icing, 162–63
Aunt Fanny's silver cake with fluffy white frosting, 65–66
Aunt Irene's fresh strawberry sherbet with almond cluster cookies, 134–36
Aunt Irene's steamed brook trout, 168
Aunt Mabel's brown stew, 102
Aunt Mae's eggless gingerbread, 251
Aunt Peg's chicken and rice pie, 78
Auntie's garden-fresh peas and baby onions, 50
Auntie's squabs with green peas, 104

B

bacon:
    in tang (summer squash dish), 168–69
    turnips with, young, 50–51
baked acorn squash topped with toasted peanuts, 218–19
baked potatoes with dill butter, 93
banana-nana-nana pudding, 44
"A Barefoot Boy" (Riley), 42
Bates, Will, 243
beef:
    in collops, old-fashioned, 103
    stew
        brown, 102
        with cornmeal dumplings, ground, 84
    see also veal
"Bendemeer's Stream" (Moore), 55
Bertie's young turnips with bacon, 50–51
"Best of All" (Riley), 152
beverages:
    mint tea, wild, 79

cheese: *see* cream cheese
cherries:
  maraschino, homemade, 160
  pie, a simple old-time, 159
"Cherry Ripe" (Eaton), 160
chicken:
  about, 73
  boiled, 63
    with Dutch dumplings, 76–77
  crispy baked, 167
  and cucumber salad with lemon
    mayonnaise, 81
  in Easter salad, 62
  easy-over oven-fried, with pan gravy,
    74–75
  gruel, 75
  hen
    boiled, with Dutch dumplings, 76–77
    boiling, 76
    for chicken and rice pie, 78
  minced roast, for little ones, 25
  pan gravy, 75
  in ramekins, 186
  and rice pie, 78
  sorghum-dipped Southern fried, 64
  stock, 74
  see also squabs
"A Child's Home—Long Ago" (Riley),
  221
chocolate:
  angel food cake, 18
  fudge glaze, 32
  fudge, velvet, 266
  icebox cookies, fruit and nut, 123
  in macaroons filled with flaked coconut,
    150
  melt-in-your-mouth cookies, 90
  in New England goodies (cookies), 195
  in Norwegian kringle, 31
  pound cake, 193
  in two-colored cookies, 58
Christmas cake, Grandma's, 269
Church, Mary Brownson, 122
"The Circus-Day Parade" (Riley), 185
cloud-light lemon sponge pudding, 28
coconut:
  cookies, 259

custard pie, 231
flaked, macaroons filled with,
  150
in icebox cookies, old-favorite, 7
coleslaw, light-green, 169
Colleen's favorite sugar cookies, 36
collops, 103
  old-fashioned, 103
confections: *see* candy
cookie crust tart shells, 199
cookies:
  almond cluster, 136
  apple, Arkansas black, 30
  apple raisin, 59
  billy goat gruff, 207
  carrot nuggets, golden, 68
  coconut, 259
  coffee cakes, old-fashioned, 211
  fruit and nut chocolate icebox, 123
  hermits, soft molasses, 96
  icebox
    fruit and nut chocolate, 123
    old-favorite, 7
  kisses, tender, 11
  kringle, Norwegian, 31
  little darlin', 129
  love knots, 9
  macaroons filled with flaked coconut,
    150
  melt-in-your-mouth chocolate, 90
  molasses hermits, soft, 96
  New England goodies, 195
  oatmeal
    peanut butter (variation), 37
    walnut, 37
  peanut butter oatmeal (variation),
    37
  star, easy-to-make, 122
  sugar, 36
  tea biscuits, old-fashioned, 19
  two-colored, 58
  walnut oatmeal, 37
  wedding-ring, 10
cornmeal:
  dumplings, 84
  egg bread, 243
  muffins, easy-to-make, 51

fancy buttered carrots, 94
a fancy watermelon salad with whipped-
      cream mayonnaise, 174
"Farmyard Song" (Trowbridge), 223
Fernald, Hannah G., 24
fish:
   broiled, with parsley and lemon butter,
      117
   carp
      à la chambord, 114
      creamed, 114
   salmon
      broiled, with parsley and lemon
         butter, 117
      creamed (substitute), 114
      deviled, with medium white sauce
         and mashed-potato meringue, 115–
         16
   soused, old-fashioned, 118
   trout, steamed brook, 168
fluffy white frosting, 66
"Folks" (Guest), 100–101
fondant, easy-to-make, 266–67
"For Christmas Day" (Turner), 56
"For the Young" (Wordsworth), 139
foxes, a tale about, 69–72
frostings:
   fluffy white, 66
   lemon cream-cheese, 57
   lemon-orange, 66
   pineapple butter, 190
   seven-minute, 213
   whipped cream, sweetened, 17
   whipped snow, 146
   see also glazes; icings; sauces, dessert
fruit:
   and nut chocolate icebox cookies, 123
   see also individual names
fudge:
   brown sugar (penuche), 267
   chocolate, velvet, 266
fudge glaze, 32

G

game: see rabbit; venison
Garland, Hamlin, 250

Gaynor, Jessie L., 265
Gertrude's favorite butter cake with
      pineapple filling and pineapple
      butter frosting, 189–90
gingerbread, eggless, 251
"Give Me the Baby" (Riley), 108
glazed ham balls in a noodle ring, 228–
      29
glazes:
   fudge, 32
   for ham balls in a noodle ring, 229
   maple-butter, 11
   powdered-sugar, a simple, 32
   see also frostings; icings; sauces, dessert
"The Golden Chance" (Guest), 85
gooseberry pie, 171
"Grace at Evening" (Guest), 26
"Grace for Light" (O'Neill), 271
graham cracker crumb topping, 259
Grandma Hoskin's red-rose honey, 210
Grandma King's patty-pan bread, 39
Grandma Meekins's mashed-potato salad,
      249
Grandma Meekins's moist-roasted Boston
      butt, 240
Grandma's Christmas cake, 269
Grandma's deluxe muffins, 157
Grandma's pumpkin custard pie with
      graham cracker crumb topping,
      258–59
Grandpa's favorite chicken-fried oysters,
      250
"Grandpa's Toy" (Titus), 268
Granny's apple raisin cookies, 59
grapes:
   in ham salad in a scalloped watermelon
      boat with lemon mayonnaise
      dressing, 176–77
gravy:
   milk, 247
   pan (chicken), 75
   for venison pot roast with vegetables,
      218
   see also sauces
ground-beef stew with cornmeal
      dumplings, 84
gruel, chicken, 75

old-fashioned one-two-three-four cake
 with lemon filling and whipped
 snow frosting, 145–46
old-fashioned soused fish, 118
old-favorite icebox cookies, 7
"Old John" (Guest), 208
"An Old Sweetheart of Mine" (Riley),
 8
"The Old-Time Family" (Guest), 48
"One, Two, Three" (Bunner), 6
O'Neill, Moira, 271
onions:
 baby, garden-fresh peas and, 50
orange-lemon frosting, 66
"Our Mother"(poem), 118
"Out Fishin'" (Guest), 111
oysters, chicken-fried, 250

P

pan gravy (chicken), 75
"Pansies" (Tapper), 21
parsley and lemon butter, 117
parsnips:
 about, 242
 pan-fried, 242
 see also turnips
pasta:
 macaroni salad, 188
 noodle ring, for glazed ham balls, 229
pastry:
 butter-crust, 236
 cookie crust tart shells, 199
 crust, sweet, 41
 double-crust, 156
 dough, tip-top, 53
 see also pies; tarts
patty pan squash: *see* squash, summer
peach:
 butter, easy-to-make early, 156
 Melba, 206–207
 nuggets, dried, 29
peanut butter oatmeal cookies (variation),
 37
peanuts:
 in melt-in-your-mouth chocolate
 cookies, 90

toasted, as topping for baked acorn
 squash, 218–19
pear:
 pie, deep-dish, 244
 salad, crunchy d'Anjou, 230
peas:
 and baby onions, garden-fresh, 50
 picking fresh, 50
 shelling, 50
 squabs with, 104
pecan(s):
 in Christmas cake, 269
 pie with butter-crust pastry, easy-to-
 make, 235–36
 toasted, 241
 in raisin-nut sauce, 241
penuche (brown sugar fudge), 267
pies:
 apple, with tip-top pastry dough, 52–
 53
 cherry, a simple old-time, 159
 coconut-custard, 231
 gooseberry, 171
 lemon meringue, 252–53
 pear, deep-dish, 244
 pecan, with butter-crust pastry, 235–36
 pumpkin custard, with graham cracker
 crumb topping, 258–59
 rhubarb, extra-special, 155
 see also pastry; tarts
pies, meat:
 chicken and rice, 78
pineapple:
 butter frosting, 190
 filling, for butter cake, 190
 in four-cup pudding, 45
"The Plaint Human" (Riley), 181
pork:
 in ham balls in a noodle ring, glazed,
 228–29
 in meat loaf, layered, 92
 sausage, in summer squash medley,
 187
 see also bacon; ham
potato(es):
 baked, with dill butter, 93
 dumplings, Dutch, 77

INDEX

INDEX

About the Author

Jane Watson Hopping lives in southwestern Oregon on an old farm place in a house that has for decades been home to dozens of children. About her are small fingerling valleys surrounded by fir and pine, and madrone-covered mountain ridges.

The author's first book, *The Pioneer Lady's Country Kitchen*, was published in 1988, her second book, *The Pioneer Lady's Country Christmas*, in 1989. Mrs. Hopping's recipes are simple: no fancy ingredients, test-tasted by generations of common folk, shared with neighbors, found tucked in other women's favorite cookbooks, or laid between the folds of a handmade quilt to be sent with a daughter to a faraway home of her own.

Jane, as the homefolks in Medford call her, is now gathering material—art, poetry, stories, recipes—for her fourth book.